DOM Enlightenment

Cody Lindley

O'REILLY®

Beijing · Cambridge · Farnham · Köln · Sebastopol · Tokyo

Table of Contents

Foreword

I make websites. Sometimes I make music. Over the years, I've noticed an interesting pattern of behavior from some musicians—often self-taught—who think of themselves as creative types: they display an aversion to learning any music theory. The logic, they say, is that knowing the theory behind music will somehow constrain their creative abilities. I've never understood that logic (and I secretly believe that it's a retroactive excuse for a lack of discipline). To my mind, I just don't see how any kind of knowledge or enlightenment could be a bad thing.

Alas, I have seen the same kind of logic at work in the world of web design. There are designers who not only don't know how to write markup and CSS, they actively refuse to learn. Again, they cite the fear of somehow being constrained by this knowledge (and again, I believe that's a self-justifying excuse).

In the world of front-end development, that attitude is fortunately far less prevalent. Most web devs understand that there's always more to learn. But even amongst developers who have an encyclopediac knowledge of HTML and CSS, there is often a knowledge gap when it comes to the Document Object Model. That's understandable. You don't need to understand the inner workings of the DOM if you're using a library like jQuery. The whole point of JavaScript libraries is to abstract away the browser's internal API and provide a different, better API instead.

Nonetheless, I think that many front-end devs have a feeling that they *should* know what's going on under the hood. That's the natural reaction of a good geek when presented with a system they're expected to work with. Now, thanks to *DOM Enlightenment*, they can scratch that natural itch.

Douglas Crockford gave us a map to understand the inner workings of the JavaScript language in his book *JavaScript: The Good Parts*. Now Cody Lindley has given us the corresponding map for the Document Object Model. Armed with this map, you'll gain the knowledge required to navigate the passageways and tunnels of the DOM.

You might not end up using this knowledge in every project. You might decide to use a library like jQuery instead. But now it will be your decision. Instead of having to use a library because that's all that you know, you can choose if and when to use a library. That's a very empowering feeling. That's what knowledge provides. That is true enlightenment.

—Jeremy Keith, founder and technical director of *clearleft.com*, and author of
DOM Scripting: Web Design with JavaScript and the Document Object Model

Preface

This book is not an exhaustive reference on DOM scripting or JavaScript (*http://javas criptenlightenment.com/*). It may, however, be the most exhaustive book written about the HTML DOM without the use of a library/framework. The lack of authorship around this topic is not without good reason. Most technical authors are not willing to wrangle this topic because of the differences that exist among legacy browsers and their implementations of the DOM specifications (or lack thereof).

For the purpose of this book (i.e., grokking the concepts), I'm going to sidestep the browser API mess and dying browser discrepancies in an effort to expose the modern DOM. That's right, I'm going to sidestep the ugliness in an effort to focus on the here and now. After all, we have solutions such as jQuery to deal with all that browser ugliness, and you should definitely be leveraging something like jQuery when dealing with deprecated browsers.

While I am not promoting the idea of only going native when it comes to DOM scripting, I did write this book in part so that developers may realize that DOM libraries are not always required when scripting the DOM. I also wrote for the lucky few who get to write JavaScript code for a single environment (i.e., one browser, mobile browsers, or HTML+CSS+JavaScript-to-native via something like PhoneGap). What you learn in this book may just make a DOM library unnecessary in ideal situations—say, for example, some light DOM scripting for deployment on a WebKit mobile browser only.

Who Should Read This Book

As I authored this book, I specifically had two types of developers in mind. I assume both types already have an intermediate to advanced knowledge of JavaScript, HTML, and CSS. The first developer is someone who has a good handle on JavaScript or jQuery, but has really never taken the time to understand the purpose and value of a library like jQuery (the reason for its rhyme, if you will). Equipped with the knowledge from this book, that developer should fully be able to understand the value provided by jQuery for scripting the DOM. And not just the value, but how jQuery abstracts the DOM and where and why jQuery is filling the gaps. The second type of developer is an engineer who is tasked with scripting HTML documents that will only run in modern browsers or that will get ported to native code for multiple OSes and device distributions (e.g., PhoneGap) and needs to avoid the overhead (i.e., size or size versus use) of a library.

Technical Intentions, Allowances, and Limitations

Before reading this book, make sure you understand the following technical intentions, allowances, and limitations:

- The content and code contained in this book was written with modern browsers (IE 9+, Firefox latest, Chrome latest, Safari latest, Opera latest) in mind. It was my goal to only include concepts and code that are native to modern browsers. If I venture outside of this goal, I will bring this fact to the readers' attention. I've generally steered away from including anything in this book that is browser-specific or implemented in a minority of the modern browsers.

- I'm not attempting in this book to dogmatically focus on a specific DOM, CSS, or HTML specification. This would be too large an undertaking (with little value, in my opinion) given the number of specifications at work and the history/status of browsers correctly implementing the specifications. I have leveraged and balanced in a very subjective manner the content from several specifications: Document Object Model (DOM) Level 3 Core Specification (*bit.ly/WYzEve*), DOM4 (*http://bit.ly/11sRdVh*), Document Object Model HTML (*http://bit.ly/UJFt0Z*), Element Traversal Specification (*http://bit.ly/11oCO12*), Selectors API Level 2 (*http://bit.ly/UJFwd8*), DOM Parsing and Serialization (*http://bit.ly/WjG8Hq*), HTML 5 Reference (*http://bit.ly/VsJ5l3*), HTML 5–A vocabulary and associated APIs for HTML and XHTML (*http://bit.ly/12ff3Zi*), HTML Living Standard (*http://bit.ly/XsT8YJ*), "HTML: The Living Standard," Developer version (*http://developers.whatwg.org/*), and DOM Living Standard (*http://dom.spec.whatwg.org/*). The content for this book is based more on where the community is and less on dogmatically attempting to express a specific spec.

- I'm covering several handpicked topics that are not DOM-specific. I've included these topics in this book to help the reader build a proper understanding of the DOM in relationship to CSS and JavaScript.

- I've purposely left out any details pertaining to XML or XHTML.

- I've purposely excluded the form and table APIs to keep the book small. But I can see these sections being added in the future.

License

The DOM Enlightenment HTML version (*http://domenlightenment.com/*) is released under a Creative Commons Attribution-Noncommercial-No Derivative Works 3.0 (*http://creativecommons.org/licenses/by-nc-nd/3.0/*) unported license.

This Book Is Not Like Other Programming Books

Before you begin, it is important to understand various styles employed in this book. Please do not skip this section, because it contains important information that will aid you in understanding these unique styles.

The Enlightenment series (also including *jQuery Enlightenment* and *JavaScript Enlightenment*) is written in a style that favors small, isolated, immediately executable code over wordy explanations and monolithic programs. One of my favorite authors, C.S. Lewis, asserts that words are the lowest form of communication that humans traffic in. I totally agree with this assertion and use it as the basis for the style of these books. I feel that technical information is best covered with as few words as possible, in conjunction with just the right amount of executable code and commenting required to express an idea. The style of this book attempts to present a clearly defined idea with as few words as possible, backed with real code. Because of this, when you first start grokking these concepts you should execute and examine the code, thereby forming the foundation of a mental model for the words used to describe the concepts. Additionally, the format of these books attempts to systematically break ideas down into their smallest possible form and examine each one in an isolated context. All of this is to say that this is not a book with lengthy explanations or in-depth coverage on broad topics. Consider yourself warned. If it helps, think of it as a cookbook, but even terser and more succinct than usual.

Color-Coding Conventions

In the code examples, bold text is used to highlight code directly relevant to the concept being discussed. Any additional code used to support the bolded code will be in normal font. Italic is reserved for comments. Here is an example:

Live code (*http://jsfiddle.net/user/domenlightenment/fiddles/*)

```
<!DOCTYPE html>
<html lang="en">
<body>
<script>

// this is a comment about a specific part of the code
var foo = 'calling out this part of the code';
```

```
</script>
</body>
</html>
```

jsFiddle

The majority of code examples in this book are linked to a corresponding jsFiddle page (*http://jsfiddle.net/*), where the code can be tweaked and executed online. The jsFiddle examples have been configured to use the Firebug lite-dev plug-in (*https://getfirebug.com/firebug-lite-debug.js*) to ensure that the reader views the *console.log* prevalent in this book. Before reading this book, make sure you are comfortable with the usage and purpose of *console.log*.

In situations where jsFiddle caused complications with the code example, I simply chose to not link to a live example.

Conventions Used in This Book

The following typographical conventions are used in this book [see also "Color-Coding Conventions" (page xiii)]:

Italic
    Indicates new terms, URLs, email addresses, filenames, and file extensions.

`Constant width`
    Used for program listings, as well as within paragraphs to refer to program elements such as variable or function names, databases, data types, environment variables, statements, and keywords.

Note
This icon signifies a tip, suggestion, or general note.

Using Code Examples

This book is here to help you get your job done. In general, if this book includes code examples, you may use the code in your programs and documentation. You do not need to contact us for permission unless you're reproducing a significant portion of the code. For example, writing a program that uses several chunks of code from this book does not require permission. Selling or distributing a CD-ROM of examples from O'Reilly books does require permission. Answering a question by citing this book and quoting example code does not require permission. Incorporating a significant amount of example code from this book into your product's documentation does require permission.

We appreciate, but do not require, attribution. An attribution usually includes the title, author, publisher, and ISBN. For example: "*DOM Enlightenment* by Cody Lindley (O'Reilly). Copyright 2013 Cody Lindley, 978-1-449-34284-5."

If you feel your use of code examples falls outside fair use or the permission given above, feel free to contact us at *permissions@oreilly.com*.

Safari® Books Online

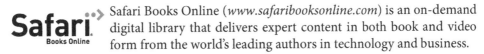 Safari Books Online (*www.safaribooksonline.com*) is an on-demand digital library that delivers expert content in both book and video form from the world's leading authors in technology and business.

Technology professionals, software developers, web designers, and business and creative professionals use Safari Books Online as their primary resource for research, problem solving, learning, and certification training.

Safari Books Online offers a range of product mixes and pricing programs for organizations, government agencies, and individuals. Subscribers have access to thousands of books, training videos, and prepublication manuscripts in one fully searchable database from publishers like O'Reilly Media, Prentice Hall Professional, Addison-Wesley Professional, Microsoft Press, Sams, Que, Peachpit Press, Focal Press, Cisco Press, John Wiley & Sons, Syngress, Morgan Kaufmann, IBM Redbooks, Packt, Adobe Press, FT Press, Apress, Manning, New Riders, McGraw-Hill, Jones & Bartlett, Course Technology, and dozens more. For more information about Safari Books Online, please visit us online.

How to Contact Us

Please address comments and questions concerning this book to the publisher:

O'Reilly Media, Inc.
1005 Gravenstein Highway North
Sebastopol, CA 95472
800-998-9938 (in the United States or Canada)
707-829-0515 (international or local)
707-829-0104 (fax)

We have a web page for this book, where we list errata, examples, and any additional information. You can access this page at *http://oreil.ly/dom-enlightenment*.

To comment or ask technical questions about this book, send email to *bookquestions@oreilly.com*.

For more information about our books, courses, conferences, and news, see our website at *http://www.oreilly.com*.

Find us on Facebook: *http://facebook.com/oreilly*

Follow us on Twitter: *http://twitter.com/oreillymedia*

Watch us on YouTube: *http://www.youtube.com/oreillymedia*

CHAPTER 1

Node Overview

1.1 The Document Object Model (a.k.a. the DOM) Is a Hierarchy/Tree of JavaScript Node Objects

When you write an HTML document, you encapsulate HTML content inside other HTML content. By doing this, you set up a hierarchy that can be expressed as a tree (*http://bit.ly/WHvXvN*). Often this hierarchy or encapsulation system is indicated visually by indenting markup in an HTML document. The browser, when loading the HTML document, interrupts and parses this hierarchy to create a tree of node objects (*http://bit.ly/VApJN5*) that simulates how the markup is encapsulated.

```
<!DOCTYPE html>
<html lang="en">
    <head>
        <title>HTML</title>
    </head>
    <body>
        <!-- Add your content here-->
    </body>
</html>
```

The preceding HTML code, when parsed by a browser, creates a document that contains nodes structured in a tree format (i.e., DOM). In Figure 1-1, I reveal the tree structure from the preceding HTML document using Opera's Dragonfly DOM Inspector.

Figure 1-1. Viewing a web page in Opera Dragonfly Developer Tools

On the left, you see the HTML document in its tree form. And on the right, you see the corresponding JavaScript object that represents the selected element on the left. For example, the selected <body> element, highlighted in blue, is an element node and an instance of the HTMLBodyElement interface.

What you should take away here is that HTML documents get parsed by a browser and converted into a tree structure of node objects representing a live document. The purpose of the DOM is to provide a programmatic interface for scripting (removing, adding, replacing, eventing, and modifying) this live document using JavaScript.

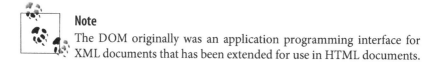

Note

The DOM originally was an application programming interface for XML documents that has been extended for use in HTML documents.

1.2 Node Object Types

Here is a list of the most common types of nodes (i.e., nodeType/node classifications) one encounters when working with HTML documents:

- DOCUMENT_NODE (e.g., window.document)
- ELEMENT_NODE (e.g., <body>, <a>, <p>, <script>, <style>, <html>, <h1>)
- ATTRIBUTE_NODE (e.g., class="funEdges")
- TEXT_NODE (e.g., text characters in an HTML document including carriage returns and whitespace)

- DOCUMENT_FRAGMENT_NODE (e.g., `document.createDocumentFragment()`)

- DOCUMENT_TYPE_NODE (e.g., `<!DOCTYPE html>`)

I've listed the node types formatted (all uppercase, with _ separating words) exactly as the constant property is written in the JavaScript browser environment as a property of the Node object. These Node properties are constant values and are used to store numeric code values that map to a specific type of node object. For example, in the following code, Node.ELEMENT_NODE is equal to 1. And 1 is the code value used to identify element nodes.

Live code (*http://jsfiddle.net/domenlightenment/BAVrs*)

```
<!DOCTYPE html>
<html lang="en">
<body>
<script>

console.log(Node.ELEMENT_NODE) /* logs 1, one is the numeric code value
                                  for element nodes */

</script>
</body>
</html>
```

In the following code I log all the node types and their values.

Live code (*http://jsfiddle.net/domenlightenment/YcXGD*)

```
<!DOCTYPE html>
<html lang="en">
<body>
<script>

for(var key in Node){
    console.log(key,' = '+Node[key]);
};

/* the above code logs to the console the following
ELEMENT_NODE  = 1
ATTRIBUTE_NODE  = 2
TEXT_NODE  = 3
CDATA_SECTION_NODE  = 4
ENTITY_REFERENCE_NODE  = 5
ENTITY_NODE  = 6
PROCESSING_INSTRUCTION_NODE  = 7
COMMENT_NODE  = 8
DOCUMENT_NODE  = 9
DOCUMENT_TYPE_NODE  = 10
DOCUMENT_FRAGMENT_NODE  = 11
NOTATION_NODE  = 12
DOCUMENT_POSITION_DISCONNECTED  = 1
```

```
DOCUMENT_POSITION_PRECEDING   = 2
DOCUMENT_POSITION_FOLLOWING   = 4
DOCUMENT_POSITION_CONTAINS    = 8
DOCUMENT_POSITION_CONTAINED_BY   = 16
DOCUMENT_POSITION_IMPLEMENTATION_SPECIFIC   = 32 */

</script>
</body>
</html>
```

The preceding code example gives an exhaustive list of all node types. For the purposes of this book, I'll be discussing the shorter list of node types shown at the start of this section. These nodes will most likely be the ones you encounter when scripting an HTML page.

In Table 1-1, I list the name given to the interface/constructor that instantiates the most common node types and their corresponding nodeType classifications by number and name. What I hope you take away from the table is that the nodeType value (i.e., 1) is just a numeric classification used to describe a certain type of node constructed from a certain JavaScript interface/constructor. For example, the HTMLBodyElement interface represents a node object that has a node type of 1, which is a classification for ELEMENT_NODEs.

Table 1-1. Node interfaces/constructors and corresponding numeric classification and name given to instances

Interface/constructor	Node (*http://bit.ly/VAqsh6*) nodeType (returned from .nodeType)
HTML*Element (*http://bit.ly/W7EPt7*) [e.g., HTMLBodyElement (*http://bit.ly/VsKSqr*)]	1 (i.e., ELEMENT_NODE)
Text (*http://bit.ly/WFG80V*)	3 (i.e., TEXT_NODE)
Attr (*http://bit.ly/WD7YOk*)	2 (i.e., ATTRIBUTE_NODE)
HTMLDocument (*http://bit.ly/12fgQNX*)	9 (i.e., DOCUMENT_NODE)
DocumentFragment (*http://bit.ly/XsVIhp*)	11 (i.e., DOCUMENT_FRAGMENT_NODE)
DocumentType (*http://bit.ly/WHxgL1*)	10 (i.e., DOCUMENT_TYPE_NODE)

Notes

The DOM specification semantically labels nodes like `Node`, `Element`, `Text`, `Attr`, and `HTMLAnchorElement` as interfaces, which they are, but keep in mind that these are also the names given to the JavaScript constructor functions that construct the nodes. As you read this book, I will be referring to these interfaces (i.e., `Element`, `Text`, `Attr`, `HTMLAnchor` `Element`) as objects or constructor functions, while the specification refers to them as interfaces.

`ATTRIBUTE_NODE` is not actually part of a tree, but rather is listed for historical reasons. In this book, I do not provide a chapter on attribute nodes and instead discuss them in Chapter 3, given that attribute nodes are sublike nodes of element nodes with no participation in the actual DOM tree structure. Be aware that the `ATTRIBUTE_NODE` is being deprecated in DOM4.

I've not included detail in this book on `COMMENT_NODE`, but you should be aware that comments in an HTML document are `Comment` nodes and are similar in nature to `Text` nodes.

As I discuss nodes throughout the book, I rarely refer to a specific node using its `nodeType` name (e.g., `ELEMENT_NODE`). This is done to be consistent with verbiage used in the specifications provided by the W3C and WHATWG.

1.3 Subnode Objects Inherit From the Node Object

Each node object in a typical DOM tree inherits properties and methods from `Node`. Depending on the type of node in the document, there are also additional subnode objects/interfaces that extend the `Node` object. The following list details the inheritance model implemented by browsers for the most common node interfaces (< indicates "inherited from"):

- `Object` < `Node` < `Element` < `HTMLElement` < (e.g., `HTML*Element`)
- `Object` < `Node` < `Attr` (this is deprecated in DOM4)
- `Object` < `Node` < `CharacterData` < `Text`
- `Object` < `Node` < `Document` < `HTMLDocument`
- `Object` < `Node` < `DocumentFragment`

It's important to remember not only that all node types inherit from `Node`, but also that the chain of inheritance can be long. For example, all `HTMLAnchorElement` nodes inherit properties and methods from `HTMLElement`, `Element`, `Node`, and `Object` objects.

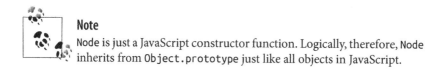

Note

Node is just a JavaScript constructor function. Logically, therefore, Node inherits from Object.prototype just like all objects in JavaScript.

To verify that all node types inherit properties and methods from the Node object, let's loop over an Element node object and examine its properties and methods (including those that are inherited).

Live code (*http://jsfiddle.net/domenlightenment/6ukxe/*)

```
<!DOCTYPE html>
<html lang="en">
<body>

<a href="#">Hi</a> <!-- this is a HTMLAnchorElement which inherits from... -->

<script>

//get reference to element node object
var nodeAnchor = document.querySelector('a');
//create props array to store property keys for element node object
var props = [];

//loop over element node object getting all properties and methods (inherited too)
for(var key in nodeAnchor){
    props.push(key);
}

//log alphabetical list of properties and methods
console.log(props.sort());

</script>
</body>
</html>
```

If you run the preceding code in a web browser, you will see a long list of properties that are available to the element node object. The properties and methods inherited from the Node object are in this list, as are a great deal of other inherited properties and methods from the Element, HTMLElement, HTMLAnchorElement, Node, and Object objects. It's not my point to examine all these properties and methods now, but rather to simply mention that all nodes inherit a set of baseline properties and methods from their constructor as well as properties from the prototype chain.

If you are more of a visual learner, consider the inheritance chain denoted from examining the previous HTML document with Opera's DOM Inspector (see Figure 1-2).

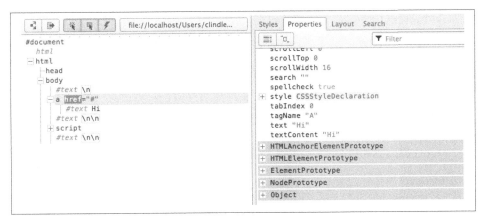

Figure 1-2. Showing node inheritance in Opera Dragonfly Developer Tools

Notice in Figure 1-2 that the anchor node inherits from `HTMLAnchorElement`, `HTMLElement`, `Element`, `Node`, and `Object`, all of which are shown in the list of properties highlighted with a gray background. This inheritance chain provides a great deal of shared methods and properties to all node types.

> **Note**
> Adding your own custom methods and properties to the DOM is possible, given the mutable and dynamic nature of JavaScript. But generally, extending host objects comes with several problems, so it's probably not a good idea to do so (*http://perfectionkills.com/whats-wrong-with-extending-the-dom/*).

1.4 Properties and Methods for Working with Nodes

As we have been discussing, all node objects (e.g., `Element`, `Attr`, `Text`, and so on) inherit properties and methods from a primary `Node` object. These properties and methods are the baseline values and functions for manipulating, inspecting, and traversing the DOM. In addition to the properties and methods provided by the node interface, a great deal of other relevant properties and methods are provided by subnode interfaces such as the `document`, `HTMLElement`, and `HTML*Element` interfaces.

The following are the most common `Node` properties and methods inherited by all node objects, including the relevant inherited properties for working with nodes from subnode interfaces.

Node properties
- `childNodes`
- `firstChild`

- lastChild

- nextSibling

- nodeName

- nodeType

- nodeValue

- parentNode

- previousSibling

Node methods
- appendChild()

- cloneNode()

- compareDocumentPosition()

- contains()

- hasChildNodes()

- insertBefore()

- isEqualNode()

- removeChild()

- replaceChild()

Document methods
- document.createElement()

- document.createTextNode()

HTML*Element *properties*
- innerHTML

- outerHTML

- textContent

- innerText

- outerText

- firstElementChild

- lastElementChild

- nextElementChild

- previousElementChild

- children

HTML element method
- `insertAdjacentHTML()`

1.5 Identifying the Type and Name of a Node

Every node has a `nodeType` and `nodeName` property that is inherited from `Node`. For example, `Text` nodes have a `nodeType` code of 3 and a `nodeName` value of `#text`. As I mentioned previously, the numeric value 3 is a numeric code representing the type of underlying object the node represents (i.e., `Node.TEXT_NODE === 3`).

Here are the values returned for `nodeType` and `nodeName` for the node objects discussed in this book. It makes sense to simply memorize these numeric codes for the more common nodes, given that we are only dealing with five numeric codes.

Live code (*http://jsfiddle.net/domenlightenment/8EwNu*)

```
<!DOCTYPE html>
<html lang="en">
<body>

<a href="#">Hi</a>

<script>

/* This is DOCUMENT_TYPE_NODE or nodeType 10
because Node.DOCUMENT_TYPE_NODE === 10 */
console.log(
    document.doctype.nodeName, /* logs 'html' also try document.doctype
                                  to get <!DOCTYPE html> */
    document.doctype.nodeType //logs 10 which maps to DOCUMENT_TYPE_NODE
);
//This is DOCUMENT_NODE or nodeType 9 because Node.DOCUMENT_NODE === 9
console.log(
    document.nodeName, //logs '#document'
    document.nodeType //logs 9 which maps to DOCUMENT_NODE
);

/* This is DOCUMENT_FRAGMENT_NODE or nodeType 11
because Node.DOCUMENT_FRAGMENT_NODE === 11 */
console.log(
    document.createDocumentFragment().nodeName, //logs '#document-fragment'
    document.createDocumentFragment().nodeType /* logs 11 which maps to
                                                  DOCUMENT_FRAGMENT_NODE */
);

//This is ELEMENT_NODE or nodeType 1 because Node. ELEMENT_NODE === 1
console.log(
    document.querySelector('a').nodeName, //logs 'A'
    document.querySelector('a').nodeType //logs 1 which maps to ELEMENT_NODE
```

```
);

//This is TEXT_NODE or nodeType 3 because Node.TEXT_NODE === 3
console.log(
    document.querySelector('a').firstChild.nodeName, //logs '#text'
    document.querySelector('a').firstChild.nodeType /* logs 3 which maps
                                            to TEXT_NODE */
);

</script>
</body>
</html>
```

In case it's not obvious, the fastest way to determine whether a node is of a certain type is to simply check its nodeType property. In the following code, I check to see if the anchor element has a node number of 1. If it does, I can conclude that it's an Element node, because Node.ELEMENT_NODE === 1.

Live code (http://jsfiddle.net/domenlightenment/ydzWL)

```
<!DOCTYPE html>
<html lang="en">
<body>

<a href="#">Hi</a>

<script>

//is <a> a ELEMENT_NODE?
console.log(document.querySelector('a').nodeType === 1); /* logs true,
                                            <a> is an Element node */

//or use Node.ELEMENT_NODE which is a property containing the numeric value of 1
console.log(document.querySelector('a').nodeType === Node.ELEMENT_NODE);
//logs true, <a> is an Element node

</script>
</body>
</html>
```

Determining the type of node you might be scripting can be very handy if you want to know which properties and methods are available to script the node.

Note

The values returned by the nodeName property vary according to the node type. See the DOM4 specification (*http://bit.ly/YIUtj9*) for details.

1.6 Getting a Node's Value

The `nodeValue` property returns `null` for most of the node types (except `Text` and `Comment`). Its use is centered on extracting actual text strings from `Text` and `Comment` nodes. In the following code, I demonstrate its use on all the nodes discussed in this book.

Live code (*http://jsfiddle.net/domenlightenment/LNyA4*)

```
<!DOCTYPE html>
<html lang="en">
<body>

<a href="#">Hi</a>

<script>

/* logs null for DOCUMENT_TYPE_NODE, DOCUMENT_NODE, DOCUMENT_FRAGMENT_NODE,
ELEMENT_NODE below */
console.log(document.doctype.nodeValue);
console.log(document.nodeValue);
console.log(document.createDocumentFragment().nodeValue);
console.log(document.querySelector('a').nodeValue);

//logs string of text
console.log(document.querySelector('a').firstChild.nodeValue); //logs 'Hi'

</script>
</body>
</html>
```

> **Note**
> `Text` or `Comment` node values can be set by providing new string values for the `nodeValue` property (i.e., `document.body.firstElement Child.nodeValue = 'hi'`).

1.7 Using JavaScript Methods to Create Element and Text Nodes

When a browser parses an HTML document, it constructs the nodes and tree based on the contents of the HTML file. The browser deals with the creation of nodes for the initial loading of the HTML document. However, it's possible to create your own nodes using JavaScript. The following two methods allow us to programmatically create `Element` and `Text` nodes using JavaScript:

- createElement()

- createTextNode()

Other methods are available but are not commonly used (e.g., createAttribute() and createComment()). In the following code, I show how simple it is to create element and text nodes.

Live code (*http://jsfiddle.net/domenlightenment/Vj2Tc*)

```
<!DOCTYPE html>
<html lang="en">
<body>
<script>

var elementNode = document.createElement('div');
console.log(elementNode, elementNode.nodeType); /* log <div> 1, and 1 indicates
                                                    an element node */

var textNode = document.createTextNode('Hi');
console.log(textNode, textNode.nodeType); /* logs Text {} 3, and 3 indicates
                                              a text node */

</script>
</body>
</html>
```

Notes

The createElement() method accepts one parameter that is a string specifying the element to be created. The string is the same string that is returned from the tagName property of an Element object.

The createAttribute() method is deprecated and should not be used for creating attribute nodes. Instead, developers typically use the get Attribute(), setAttribute(), and removeAttribute() methods. I will discuss this in more detail in Chapter 3.

The createDocumentFragment() method will be discussed in Chapter 8.

You should be aware that a createComment() method is available for creating comment nodes. It's not discussed in this book, but is available to any developer who finds its usage valuable.

1.8 Using JavaScript Strings to Create and Add Element and Text Nodes to the DOM

The innerHTML, outerHTML, textContent, and insertAdjacentHTML() properties and methods provide the functionality to create and add nodes to the DOM using JavaScript strings.

In the following code, I am using the innerHTML, outerHTML, and textContent properties to create nodes from JavaScript strings that are then immediately added to the DOM.

Live code (*http://jsfiddle.net/domenlightenment/UrNT3*)

```
<!DOCTYPE html>
<html lang="en">
<body>

<div id="A"></div>
<span id="B"></span>
<div id="C"></div>
<div id="D"></div>
<div id="E"></div>

<script>

//create a strong element and text node and add it to the DOM
document.getElementById('A').innerHTML = '<strong>Hi</strong>';

/* create a div element and text node to replace <span id="B"></div>
(notice span#B is replaced) */
document.getElementById('B').outerHTML = '<div id="B"
    class="new">Whats Shaking</div>'

//create a text node and update the div#C with the text node
document.getElementById('C').textContent = 'dude';


//NON standard extensions below i.e., innerText and outerText

//create a text node and update the div#D with the text node
document.getElementById('D').innerText = 'Keep it';

/* create a text node and replace the div#E with the text node
(notice div#E is gone) */
document.getElementById('E').outerText = 'real!';
```

```
console.log(document.body.innerHTML);
/* logs
<div id="A"><strong>Hi</strong></div>
<div id="B" class="new">Whats Shaking</div>
<span id="C">dude</span>
<div id="D">Keep it</div>
real!
*/

</script>
</body>
</html>
```

The insertAdjacentHTML() method, which only works on Element nodes, is a good deal more precise than the previously mentioned methods. Using this method, it's possible to insert nodes before the beginning tag, after the beginning tag, before the end tag, and after the end tag. In the following code, I construct a sentence using the insertAdjacentHTML() method.

Live code (*http://jsfiddle.net/domenlightenment/tvpA6*)

```
<!DOCTYPE html>
<html lang="en">
<body><i id="elm">how</i>

<script>

var elm = document.getElementById('elm');

elm.insertAdjacentHTML('beforebegin', '<span>Hey-</span>');
elm.insertAdjacentHTML('afterbegin', '<span>dude-</span>');
elm.insertAdjacentHTML('beforeend', '<span>-are</span>');
elm.insertAdjacentHTML('afterend', '<span>-you?</span>');

console.log(document.body.innerHTML);
/* logs
<span>Hey-</span><i id="A"><span>dude-</span>how<span>-are</span></i>
<span>-you?</span>
*/

</script>
</body>
</html>
```

Notes

The `innerHTML` property will convert HTML elements found in the string to actual DOM nodes, while `textContent` can only be used to construct text nodes. If you pass `textContent` a string containing HTML elements, it will simply spit it out as text.

`document.write()` can also be used to simultaneously create and add nodes to the DOM. However, it's typically not used unless its usage is required to accomplish third-party scripting tasks. Basically, the `write()` method will output to the page the values passed to it during page loading/parsing. You should be aware that using the `write()` method will stall/block the parsing of the HTML document being loaded.

`innerHTML` invokes a heavy and expensive HTML parser, whereas text node generation is trivial; thus, use `innerHTML` and friends sparingly.

The `insertAdjacentHTML` options `beforebegin` and `afterend` will only work if the node is in the DOM tree and has a parent element.

Support for `outerHTML` was not available natively in Firefox until version 11. A polyfill (*https://gist.github.com/1044128*) is available.

`textContent` gets the content of all elements, including `<script>` and `<style>` elements, but `innerText` does not.

`innerText` is aware of style and will not return the text of hidden elements, whereas `textContent` will.

Available to all modern browsers except Firefox are `insertAdjacentElement()` and `insertAdjacentText()`.

1.9 Extracting Parts of the DOM Tree as JavaScript Strings

Exactly the same properties (`innerHTML`, `outerHTML`, `textContent`) that we use to create and add nodes to the DOM can also be used to extract parts of the DOM (or really, the entire DOM) as a JavaScript string. In the following code example, I use these properties to return a string value containing text and HTML values from the HTML document.

Live code (*http://jsfiddle.net/domenlightenment/mMYWc*)

```
<!DOCTYPE html>
<html lang="en">
<body>

<div id="A"><i>Hi</i></div>
<div id="B">Dude<strong> !</strong></div>

<script>

console.log(document.getElementById('A').innerHTML); //logs '<i>Hi</i>'
```

```
console.log(document.getElementById('A').outerHTML); /* logs
                                    <div id="A">Hi</div> */

/* notice that all text is returned even if it's in child element nodes
(i.e., <strong> !</strong>) */
console.log(document.getElementById('B').textContent); //logs 'Dude !'

//NON standard extensions below i.e., innerText and outerText

console.log(document.getElementById('B').innerText); //logs 'Dude !'

console.log(document.getElementById('B').outerText); //logs 'Dude !'

</script>
</body>
</html>
```

 Note
The textContent, innerText, and outerText properties, when being read, will return all the text nodes contained within the selected node. So, as an example (note that this is not a good idea in practice), docu ment.body.textContent will get all the text nodes contained in the body element, not just the first text node.

1.10 Using appendChild() and insertBefore() to Add Node Objects to the DOM

The appendChild() and insertBefore() node methods allow us to insert JavaScript node objects into the DOM tree. The appendChild() method will append a node (or multiple nodes) to the end of the child node(s) of the node the method is called on. If there is no child node(s), the node being appended is appended as the first child. For example in the following code, I am creating an element node (<strong>) and a text node (Dude). Then the <p> element is selected from the DOM and the <strong> element is appended using appendChild(). Notice that the <strong> element is encapsulated inside the <p> element and added as the last child node. Next, the <strong> element is selected and the text Dude is appended to the <strong> element.

Live code (*http://jsfiddle.net/domenlightenment/HxjFt*)

```
<!DOCTYPE html>
<html lang="en">
<body>

<p>Hi</p>

<script>
```

```
//create a blink element node and text node
var elementNode = document.createElement('strong');
var textNode = document.createTextNode(' Dude');

//append these nodes to the DOM
document.querySelector('p').appendChild(elementNode);
document.querySelector('strong').appendChild(textNode);

//log's <p>Hi<strong> Dude</strong></p>
console.log(document.body.innerHTML);

</script>
</body>
</html>
```

When it becomes necessary to control the location of insertion beyond appending nodes to the end of a child list of nodes, we can use `insertBefore()`. In the following code, I am inserting the `<li>` element before the first child node of the `<ul>` element.

Live code (*http://jsfiddle.net/domenlightenment/UmkME*)

```
<!DOCTYPE html>
<html lang="en">
<body>

<ul>
    <li>2</li>
    <li>3</li>
</ul>

<script>

//create a text node and li element node and append the text to the li
var text1 = document.createTextNode('1');
var li = document.createElement('li');
li.appendChild(text1);

//select the ul in the document
var ul = document.querySelector('ul');

/*
add the li element we created above to the DOM, notice I call on <ul>
and pass reference to <li>2</li> using ul.firstChild
*/
ul.insertBefore(li,ul.firstChild);

console.log(document.body.innerHTML);
/*logs
<ul>
<li>1</li>
<li>2</li>
```

```
<li>3</li>
</ul>
*/

</script>
</body>
</html>
```

The insertBefore() method requires two parameters: the node to be inserted and the reference node in the document before which you would like the node inserted.

Note

If you do not pass a second parameter to the insertBefore() method, then it functions just like appendChild().

We have more methods (e.g., prepend(), append(), before(), and af ter()) to look forward to in DOM4 (*http://www.w3.org/TR/dom/ #mutation-methods*).

1.11 Using removeChild() and replaceChild() to Remove and Replace Nodes

Removing a node from the DOM is a bit of a multistep process. First you have to select the node you want to remove. Then you need to gain access to its parent element, typically by using the parentNode property. It's on the parent node that you invoke the removeChild() method, passing it the reference to the node to be removed. Here I demonstrate its use on an element node and a text node.

Live code (*http://jsfiddle.net/domenlightenment/VDZgP*)

```
<!DOCTYPE html>
<html lang="en">
<body>

<div id="A">Hi</div>
<div id="B">Dude</div>

<script>

//remove element node
var divA = document.getElementById('A');
divA.parentNode.removeChild(divA);

//remove text node
var divB = document.getElementById('B').firstChild;
divB.parentNode.removeChild(divB);
```

```
//log the new DOM updates, which should only show the remaining empty div#B
console.log(document.body.innerHTML);

</script>
</body>
</html>
```

Replacing an element or text node is not unlike removing one. In the following code, I use the same HTML structure as in the preceding code example, except this time, I use replaceChild() to update the nodes instead of removing them.

Live code (*http://jsfiddle.net/domenlightenment/zgE8M*)

```
<!DOCTYPE html>
<html lang="en">
<body>

<div id="A">Hi</div>
<div id="B">Dude</div>

<script>

//replace element node
var divA = document.getElementById('A');
var newSpan = document.createElement('span');
newSpan.textContent = 'Howdy';
divA.parentNode.replaceChild(newSpan,divA);

//replace text node
var divB = document.getElementById('B').firstChild;
var newText = document.createTextNode('buddy');
divB.parentNode.replaceChild(newText, divB);

//log the new DOM updates
console.log(document.body.innerHTML);

</script>
</body>
</html>
```

1.12 Using cloneNode() to Clone Nodes

Using the cloneNode() method, it's possible to duplicate a single node or a node and all its child nodes.

In the following code, I clone only the <ul> (i.e., HTMLULListElement) that, once cloned, can be treated like any node reference.

Live code (*http://jsfiddle.net/domenlightenment/6DHgC*)

```
<!DOCTYPE html>
<html lang="en">
<body>

<ul>
  <li>Hi</li>
  <li>there</li>
</ul>

<script>

var cloneUL = document.querySelector('ul').cloneNode();

console.log(cloneUL.constructor); //logs HTMLULListElement()
console.log(cloneUL.innerHTML); //logs (an empty string) as only the ul was cloned

</script>
</body>
</html>
```

To clone a node and all its child nodes, you pass the cloneNode() method a parameter of true. The following code uses the cloneNode() method again, but this time, I am cloning all the child nodes as well.

```
<!DOCTYPE html>
<html lang="en">
<body>

<ul>
  <li>Hi</li>
  <li>there</li>
</ul>

<script>

var cloneUL = document.querySelector('ul').cloneNode(true);

console.log(cloneUL.constructor); //logs HTMLUListElement()
console.log(cloneUL.innerHTML); //logs <li>Hi</li><li>there</li>

</script>
</body>
</html>
```

Note

When cloning an Element node, all of its attributes and their values (including in-line events) are cloned as well. Anything added with ad dEventListener() or node.onclick is not cloned.

You might think that cloning a node and its children using clone Node(true) would return a NodeList, but it in fact does not.

cloneNode() may lead to duplicate element IDs in a document.

1.13 Grokking Node Collections (i.e., NodeList and HTMLCollection)

When selecting groups of nodes from a tree (see Chapter 3) or accessing predefined sets of nodes, the nodes are placed in either a NodeList (*http://www.w3.org/TR/dom/#nodel ist*) [e.g., document.querySelectorAll('*')] or an HTMLCollection (*http:// www.w3.org/TR/dom/#htmlcollection*) (e.g., document.scripts). These array-like object collections have the following characteristics:

- A collection can be either live or static. This means the nodes contained in the collection are either literally part of the live document or a snapshot of the live document.

- By default, nodes are sorted inside the collection by tree order. This means the order matches the linear path from tree trunk to branches.

- The collections have a `length` property that reflects the number of elements in the list.

1.14 Getting a List/Collection of All Immediate Child Nodes

Using the `childNodes` property produces an array-like list [i.e., `NodeList` (*https://devel oper.mozilla.org/En/DOM/NodeList*)] of the immediate child nodes. In the following code, I select the `<ul>` element, which I then use to create a list of all the immediate child nodes contained inside the `<ul>`.

Live code (*http://jsfiddle.net/domenlightenment/amDev*)

```
<!DOCTYPE html>
<html lang="en">
<body>

<ul>
  <li>Hi</li>
  <li>there</li>
</ul>

<script>

var ulElementChildNodes = document.querySelector('ul').childNodes;

console.log(ulElementChildNodes); /* logs an arraylike list of all nodes
                                     inside of the ul */

/* Call forEach as if it's a method of NodeLists so we can loop over the NodeList.
Done because NodeLists are arraylike, but do not directly inherit from Array */
Array.prototype.forEach.call(ulElementChildNodes,function(item){
    console.log(item); //logs each item in the array
});

</script>
</body>
</html>
```

 Notes

The `NodeList` returned by `childNodes` only contains immediate child nodes.

Be aware that `childNodes` contains not only `Element` nodes but also all other node types (e.g., `Text` and `Comment` nodes).

`[].forEach` was implemented in ECMAScript Edition 5.

1.15 Converting a NodeList or HTMLCollection to a JavaScript Array

Node lists and HTML collections are array-like but are not true JavaScript arrays, which inherit array methods. In the following code, I programmatically confirm this using isArray().

Live code (*http://jsfiddle.net/domenlightenment/n53Xk*)

```
<!DOCTYPE html>
<html lang="en">
<body>

<a href="#"></a>

<script>

console.log(Array.isArray(document.links)); /* returns false, it's an
                                    HTMLCollection not an Array */
console.log(Array.isArray(document.querySelectorAll('a'))); /* returns false, it's
                                                a NodeList not an
                                                Array */

</script>
</body>
</html>
```

Note

Array.isArray was implemented in ECMAScript Edition 5.

Converting a node list and HTML collection list to a true JavaScript array can provide several benefits. For one, it gives us the ability to create a snapshot of the list that is not tied to the live DOM, considering that NodeList and HTMLCollection are live lists (*http://bit.ly/Xt1Y95*). Second, converting a list to a JavaScript array gives access to the methods provided by the Array object (e.g., forEach, pop, map, reduce, and so on.).

To convert an array-like list to a true JavaScript array we pass the array-like list to call() or apply(), in which the call() or apply() is calling a method that returns an unaltered true JavaScript array. In the following code, I use the .slice() method, which doesn't really slice anything; I am just using it to convert the list to a JavaScript Array since the slice() returns an array.

Live code (*http://jsfiddle.net/domenlightenment/jHgTY*)

```
<!DOCTYPE html>
<html lang="en">
<body>
```

```
<a href="#"></a>

<script>

console.log(Array.isArray(Array.prototype.slice.call(document.links)));
    //returns true
console.log(Array.isArray(
    Array.prototype.slice.call(document.querySelectorAll('a')))); //returns true

</script>
</body>
</html>
```

Notes

In ECMAScript Edition 6, we have Array.from to look forward to, which converts a single argument that is an array-like object or list (e.g., arguments, NodeList, DOMTokenList [used by classList], and NamedNodeMap [used by the attributes property]) into a new Array() and returns it.

1.16 Traversing Nodes in the DOM

From a node reference (i.e., document.querySelector('ul')), it's possible to get a different node reference by traversing the DOM using the following properties:

- parentNode
- firstChild
- lastChild
- nextSibling
- previousSibling

In the following code example, I examine the Node properties providing DOM traversal functionality.

Live code (*http://jsfiddle.net/domenlightenment/Hvfhv*)

```
<!DOCTYPE html>
<html lang="en">
<body><ul><!-- comment -->
<li id="A"></li>
<li id="B"></li>
<!-- comment -->
</ul>

<script>
```

```
//cache selection of the ul
var ul = document.querySelector('ul');

//What is the parentNode of the ul?
console.log(ul.parentNode.nodeName); //logs body

//What is the first child of the ul?
console.log(ul.firstChild.nodeName); //logs comment

//What is the last child of the ul?
console.log(ul.lastChild.nodeName); /* logs text not comment,
                                    because there is a line break */

//What is the nextSibling of the first li?
console.log(ul.querySelector('#A').nextSibling.nodeName); //logs text

//What is the previousSibling of the last li?
console.log(ul.querySelector('#B').previousSibling.nodeName); //logs text

</script>
</body>
</html>
```

If you are familiar with the DOM, you should not be surprised that traversing the DOM includes traversing not just element nodes, but also text and comment nodes (I believe the preceding code example makes this clear), and this is not exactly ideal. Using the following properties we can traverse the DOM, while ignoring text and comment nodes:

- firstElementChild
- lastElementChild
- nextElementChild
- previousElementChild
- children
- parentElement

Note

The childElementCount is not mentioned, but you should be aware of its availability for calculating the number of child elements a node contains.

Let's examine our code example again using only element traversing methods.

Live code (*http://jsfiddle.net/domenlightenment/Wh7nf*)

```html
<!DOCTYPE html>
<html lang="en">
<body><ul><!-- comment -->
<li id="A">foo</li>
<li id="B">bar</li>
<!-- comment -->
</ul>

<script>

//cache selection of the ul
var ul = document.querySelector('ul');

//What is the first child of the ul?
console.log(ul.firstElementChild.nodeName); //logs li

//What is the last child of the ul?
console.log(ul.lastElementChild.nodeName); //logs li

//What is the nextSibling of the first li?
console.log(ul.querySelector('#A').nextElementSibling.nodeName); //logs li

//What is the previousSibling of the last li?
console.log(ul.querySelector('#B').previousElementSibling.nodeName); //logs li

//What are the element only child nodes of the ul?
console.log(ul.children); //HTMLCollection, all child nodes including text nodes

//What is the parent element of the first li?
console.log(ul.firstElementChild.parentElement); //logs ul

</script>
</body>
</html>
```

1.17 Verifying a Node Position in the DOM Tree with contains() and compareDocumentPosition()

It's possible to know whether a node is contained inside another node by using the contains() node method. In the following code I ask if <body> is contained inside <html lang="en">.

Live code (*http://jsfiddle.net/domenlightenment/ENU4w*)

```html
<!DOCTYPE html>
<html lang="en">
<body>

<script>
```

```
// is <body> inside <html lang="en"> ?
var inside =
  document.querySelector('html').contains(document.querySelector('body'));

console.log(inside); //logs true

</script>
</body>
</html>
```

If you need more robust information about the position of a node in the DOM tree in regard to the nodes around it, you can use the compareDocumentPosition() node method. Basically, this method gives you the ability to request information about a selected node relative to the node passed in. The information that you get back is a number that corresponds to the information shown in Table 1-2.

Table 1-2. The meaning of the numeric values returned from compareDocumentPosition()

Number code returned from compareDocumentPosition()	Number code information
0	Elements are identical.
1	DOCUMENT_POSITION_DISCONNECTED Set when selected node and passed-in node are not in the same document.
2	DOCUMENT_POSITION_PRECEDING Set when passed-in node is preceding selected node.
4	DOCUMENT_POSITION_FOLLOWING Set when passed-in node is following selected node.
8	DOCUMENT_POSITION_CONTAINS Set when passed-in node is an ancestor of selected node.
16, 10	DOCUMENT_POSITION_CONTAINED_BY (16, 10 in hexadecimal) Set when passed-in node is a descendant of selected node.

Notes

contains() will return true if the node selected and the node passed in are identical.

compareDocumentPosition() can be rather confusing, because it's possible for a node to have more than one type of relationship with another node. For example, when a node both contains (16) and precedes (4), the returned value from compareDocumentPosition() will be 20.

1.18 Determining Whether Two Nodes Are Identical

According to the DOM3 specification (*http://bit.ly/TlJjOl*), two nodes are equal if and only if the following conditions are satisfied:

- The two nodes are of the same type.
- The following string attributes are equal: nodeName, localName, namespaceURI, prefix, and nodeValue. That is, they are both null, or they have the same length and are identical character for character.
- The attributes NamedNodeMaps are equal. That is, they are both null, or they have the same length and for each node that exists in one map, there is a node that exists in the other map and is equal, although not necessarily at the same index.
- The childNodes NodeLists are equal. That is, they are both null, or they have the same length and contain equal nodes at the same index. Note that normalization can affect equality; to avoid this, nodes should be normalized before being compared.

Calling the isEqualNode() method on a node in the DOM will ask if that node is equal to the node that you pass it as a parameter. In the following code, I exhibit a case of two identical nodes and two nodes that do not meet the conditions of being equal to each other.

Live code (*http://jsfiddle.net/domenlightenment/xw68Q*)

```
<!DOCTYPE html>
<html lang="en">
<body>

<input type="text">
<input type="text">

<textarea>foo</textarea>
<textarea>bar</textarea>

<script>

//logs true, because they are exactly identical
var input = document.querySelectorAll('input');
console.log(input[0].isEqualNode(input[1]));

//logs false, because the child text node is not the same
var textarea = document.querySelectorAll('textarea');
console.log(textarea[0].isEqualNode(textarea[1]));

</script>
</body>
</html>
```

Note

If you don't care about two nodes being exactly equal, and instead you want to know whether two node references refer to the same node, you can simply check them using the === operator (i.e., `document.body` === `document.body`). This will tell you if they are identical but not equal.

CHAPTER 2

Document Nodes

2.1 document Node Overview

The `HTMLDocument` constructor (which inherits from document) creates a DOCU MENT_NODE (i.e., a `window.document`) in the DOM. To verify this, I can simply ask which constructor was used in the creation of the document node object.

Live code (*http://jsfiddle.net/domenlightenment/qRAzL*)

```
<!DOCTYPE html>
<html lang="en">
<body>
<script>

console.log(window.document.constructor); /* logs function HTMLDocument()
                                  { [native code] } */
console.log(window.document.nodeType); /* logs 9, which is a numeric key
                                  mapping to DOCUMENT_NODE */

</script>
</body>
</html>
```

The preceding code concludes that the `HTMLDocument` constructor function constructs the `window.document` node object and that this node is a DOCUMENT_NODE object.

Note

Both Document and HTMLDocument constructors are typically instantiated by the browser when you load an HTML document. However,
using document.implementation.createHTMLDocument(), it's possible
to create your own HTML document outside the one currently loaded
in the browser. In addition to createHTMLDocument(), it's possible to
create a document object that has yet to be set up as an HTML document
using createDocument(). An example use of these methods might be
to programmatically provide an HTML document to an iframe.

2.2 HTMLDocument Properties and Methods (Including Inherited)

To get accurate information pertaining to the available properties and methods on an
HTMLDocument node, it's best to ignore the specification and to ask the browser what is
available. Examine the arrays created in the following code detailing the properties and
methods available from an HTMLDocument node (a.k.a. window.document) object.

Live code (*http://jsfiddle.net/domenlightenment/jprPe*)

```
<!DOCTYPE html>
<html lang="en">
<body>
<script>

//document own properties
console.log(Object.keys(document).sort());

//document own properties and inherited properties
var documentPropertiesIncludeInherited = [];
for(var p in document){
    documentPropertiesIncludeInherited.push(p);
}
console.log(documentPropertiesIncludeInherited.sort());

//documment inherited properties only
var documentPropertiesOnlyInherited = [];
for(var p in document){
    if(
        !document.hasOwnProperty(p)){documentPropertiesOnlyInherited.push(p);
    }
}
console.log(documentPropertiesOnlyInherited.sort());

</script>
</body>
</html>
```

Many properties are available, even if the inherited properties were not considered. I've handpicked a list of noteworthy properties and methods for the context of this chapter:

- doctype
- documentElement
- implementation.*
- activeElement
- body
- head
- title
- lastModified
- referrer
- URL
- defaultview
- compatMode
- ownerDocument
- hasFocus()

Note

The HTMLDocument node object (i.e., window.document) is used to access a great deal of the methods and properties available for working with the DOM (i.e., document.querySelectorAll()). Many of the properties that we do not cover in this chapter are discussed elsewhere in the book.

2.3 Getting General HTML Document Information (title, url, referrer, lastModified, and compatMode)

The document object provides access to some general information about the HTML document/DOM being loaded. In the following code, I use the document.title, document.URL, document.referrer, document.lastModified, and document.compatMode properties to gain some general information about the document. Based on the property name, the returned values should be obvious.

Live code (*http://jsfiddle.net/domenlightenment/pX8Le*)

```html
<!DOCTYPE html>
<html lang="en">
<body>
<script>

var d = document;
console.log('title = ' +d.title);
console.log('url = ' +d.URL);
console.log('referrer = ' +d.referrer);
console.log('lastModified = ' +d.lastModified);

//logs either BackCompat (Quirks Mode) or CSS1Compat (Strict Mode)
console.log('compatibility mode = ' +d.compatMode);

</script>
</body>
</html>
```

2.4 document Child Nodes

document nodes can contain one DocumentType node object and one Element node object. This should not be a surprise, since HTML documents typically contain only one doctype (e.g., <!DOCTYPE html>) and one element (e.g., <html lang="en">). Thus, if you ask for the children (e.g., document.childNodes) of the document object, you will get an array containing, at the very least, the document's doctype/DTD and <html lang="en"> element. The following code showcases the fact that window.document is a type of node object (i.e., Document) with child nodes.

Live code (*http://jsfiddle.net/domenlightenment/UasKc*)

```html
<!DOCTYPE html>
<html lang="en">
<body>
<script>
//This is the doctype/DTD
console.log(document.childNodes[0].nodeType); /* logs 10, which is a numeric key
                                                 mapping to DOCUMENT_TYPE_NODE */

//This is the <html> element
console.log(document.childNodes[1].nodeType); /* logs 1, which is a numeric key
                                                 mapping to ELEMENT_TYPE_NODE */

</script>
</body>
</html>
```

Notes

Don't confuse the `window.document` object created from the `HTMLDocu`ment constructor with the `Document` object. Just remember that `window.document` is the starting point for the DOM interface. That is why `document.childNodes` contains child nodes.

If a comment node (not discussed in this book) is made outside the `<html lang="en">` element, it will become a child node of the `win`dow.document. However, having comment nodes outside the `<html>` element can cause some buggy results in IE and is a violation of the DOM specification.

2.5 document Provides Shortcuts to <!DOCTYPE>, <html lang="en">, <head>, and <body>

Using the following properties, we can get a shortcut reference to the following nodes:

- `document.doctype` refers to `<!DOCTYPE>`.
- `document.documentElement` refers to `<html lang="en">`.
- `document.head` refers to `<head>`.
- `document.body` refers to `<body>`.

This is demonstrated in the following code.

Live code (*http://jsfiddle.net/domenlightenment/XsSTM*)

```
<!DOCTYPE html>
<html lang="en">
<body>
<script>

console.log(document.doctype); /* logs DocumentType {nodeType=10,
                                  ownerDocument=document, ...} */

console.log(document.documentElement); // logs <html lang="en">

console.log(document.head); // logs <head>

console.log(document.body); // logs <body>

</script>

</body>
</html>
```

Note

The doctype or DTD is a nodeType of 10 or `DOCUMENT_TYPE_NODE` and should not be confused with the `DOCUMENT_NODE` (a.k.a. `window.docu ment` constructed from `HTMLDocument()`). The doctype is constructed from the `DocumentType()` constructor.

In Safari, Chrome, and Opera, the `document.doctype` does not appear in the `document.childNodes` list.

2.6 Using document.implementation.hasFeature() to Detect DOM Specifications/Features

It's possible, using `document.implementation.hasFeature()`, to ask the current document (for a boolean) what feature and level the browser has implemented/supports. For example, we can ask if the browser has implemented the Core DOM Level 3 specification by passing the name of the feature and the version to the `hasFeature()` method. In the following code, I ask if the browser has implemented the Core 2.0 and 3.0 specifications.

Live code (*http://jsfiddle.net/domenlightenment/TYYZ6*)

```
<!DOCTYPE html>
<html lang="en">
<body>
<script>

console.log(document.implementation.hasFeature('Core','2.0'));
console.log(document.implementation.hasFeature('Core','3.0'));

</script>
</body>
</html>
```

Table 2-1 defines the features [the spec calls these *modules* (*http://bit.ly/14vfuNS*)] and versions to which you can pass the `hasFeature()` method.

Table 2-1. hasFeature() parameter values

Feature	Supported versions
Core	1.0, 2.0, 3.0
XML	1.0, 2.0, 3.0
HTML	1.0, 2.0
Views	2.0
StyleSheets	2.0
CSS	2.0
CSS2	2.0

Feature	Supported versions
Events	2.0, 3.0
UIEvents	2.0, 3.0
MouseEvents	2.0, 3.0
MutationEvents	2.0, 3.0
HTMLEvents	2.0
Range	2.0
Traversal	2.0
LS (loading and saving between files and DOM trees synchronously)	3.0
LS-Async (loading and saving between files and DOM trees asynchronously)	3.0
Validation	3.0

Notes

Don't trust hasFeature() alone; you should use capability detection (*http://bit.ly/XcI54f*) in addition to hasFeature().

Using the isSupported method, implementation information can be gathered for a specific/selected node only (i.e., element.isSupported(feature,version).

You can determine online what a user agent supports. On this site, (*http://www.w3.org/2003/02/06-dom-support.html*) you will find a table indicating what the browser loading the URL claims to implement.

2.7 Getting a Reference to the Focus/Active Node in the Document

Using the document.activeElement, we can quickly get a reference to the node in the document that is focused/active. In the following code, on page load, I am setting the focus of the document to the <textarea> node and then gaining a reference to that node by using the activeElement property.

Live code (*http://jsfiddle.net/domenlightenment/N9npb*)

```
<!DOCTYPE html>
<html lang="en">
<body>
<textarea></textarea>

<script>

//set focus to <textarea>
document.querySelector('textarea').focus();
```

```
//get reference to element that is focused/active in the document
console.log(document.activeElement); //logs <textarea>

</script>
</body>
</html>
```

Note
The focused/active element returns elements that have the ability to be focused. If you visit a web page in a browser and start pressing the Tab key, you will see focus shifting from one element to another element in the page that can receive focus. Don't confuse the selection of nodes (highlighting sections of the HTML page with your mouse) with elements that get focus for the purpose of inputting something with keystrokes, the space bar, or a mouse.

2.8 Determining Whether the Document or Any Node Inside the Document Has Focus

Using the document.hasFocus() method, it's possible to know whether the user currently is focused on the window that has the HTML document loaded. In the following code, you can see that if I execute the code and then focus another window, tab, or application all together, getFocus() will return false.

Live code (*http://jsfiddle.net/domenlightenment/JkE3d*)

```
<!DOCTYPE html>
<html lang="en">
<body>

<script>

/* If you keep focus on the window/tab that has the document loaded it's true.
If not it's false. */
setTimeout(function(){console.log(document.hasFocus())},5000);

</script>
</body>
</html>
```

2.9 document.defaultView Is a Shortcut to the Head/ Global Object

You should be aware that the defaultView property is a shortcut to the JavaScript head object, or what some refer to as the global object. The head object in a web browser is the `window` object, and `defaultView` will point to this object in a JavaScript browser enviroment. The following code demonstrates the value of `defaultView` in a browser.

Live code (*http://jsfiddle.net/domenlightenment/QqK6Q*)

```
<!DOCTYPE html>
<html lang="en">
<body>
<script>

console.log(document.defaultView) //reference, head JS object.
                                  Would be window object in a browser. */

</script>
</body>
</html>
```

If you are dealing with a DOM that is headless or a JavaScript environment that is not running in a web browser [i.e., Node.js (*http://nodejs.org/*)], this property can get you access to the head object scope.

2.10 Using ownerDocument to Get a Reference to the Document from an Element

The `ownerDocument` property, when called on a node, returns a reference to the docu ment within which the node is contained. In the following code, I get a reference to the document of the <body> in the HTML document and the document node for the <body> element contained inside the iframe.

Live code: N/A

```
<!DOCTYPE html>
<html lang="en">
<body>

<iframe src="http://someFileServedFromServerOnSameDomain.html"></iframe>

<script>

//get the window.document that the <body> is contained within
console.log(document.body.ownerElement);

//get the window.document the <body> inside of the iframe is contained within
console.log(window.frames[0].document.body.ownerElement);

</script>
</body>
</html>
```

If `ownerDocument` is called on the document node, the value returned is `null`.

CHAPTER 3

Element Nodes

3.1 HTML*Element Object Overview

Each element in an HTML document has a unique nature, and as such, each has a unique JavaScript constructor (*http://bit.ly/UJFt0Z*) that instantiates the element as a node object in a DOM tree. For example, an `<a>` element is created as a DOM node from the `HTMLAnchorElement()` constructor. In the following code, I verify that an anchor element is created from `HTMLAnchorElement()`.

Live code (*http://jsfiddle.net/domenlightenment/TgcNu*)

```
<!DOCTYPE html>
<html lang="en">
<body>

<a></a>

<script>
/* grab <a> element node from DOM and ask for the name of the constructor
that constructed it */
console.log(document.querySelector('a').constructor);
//logs function HTMLAnchorElement() { [native code] }

</script>
</body>
</html>
```

In the preceding code example, I am trying to make the point that each element in the DOM is constructed from a unique JavaScript interface/constructor. The following list should give you a good sense of the interfaces/constructors used to create HTML elements.

HTMLHtmlElement	HTMLParagraphElement
HTMLHeadElement	HTMLHeadingElement

```
HTMLLinkElement                HTMLQuoteElement
HTMLTitleElement               HTMLPreElement
HTMLMetaElement                HTMLBRElement
HTMLBaseElement                HTMLBaseFontElement
HTMLIsIndexElement             HTMLFontElement
HTMLStyleElement               HTMLHRElement
HTMLBodyElement                HTMLModElement
HTMLFormElement                HTMLAnchorElement
HTMLSelectElement              HTMLImageElement
HTMLOptGroupElement            HTMLObjectElement
HTMLOptionElement              HTMLParamElement
HTMLInputElement               HTMLAppletElement
HTMLTextAreaElement            HTMLMapElement
HTMLButtonElement              HTMLAreaElement
HTMLLabelElement               HTMLScriptElement
HTMLFieldSetElement            HTMLTableElement
HTMLLegendElement              HTMLTableCaptionElement
HTMLUListElement               HTMLTableColElement
HTMLOListElement               HTMLTableSectionElement
HTMLDListElement               HTMLTableRowElement
HTMLDirectoryElement           HTMLTableCellElement
HTMLMenuElement                HTMLFrameSetElement
HTMLLIElement                  HTMLFrameElement
HTMLDivElement                 HTMLIFrameElement
```

The complete list is available here (*http://bit.ly/YIV4RR*). Keep in mind that each
HTML*Element in the preceding list inherits properties and methods from HTMLEle
ment, Element, Node, and Object.

3.2 HTML*Element Object Properties and Methods (Including Inherited)

To get accurate information pertaining to the available properties and methods on an
HTML*Element node, it's best to ignore the specification and to ask the browser what is
available. Examine the arrays created in the following code detailing the properties and
methods available from HTML element nodes.

Live code (*http://jsfiddle.net/domenlightenment/vZUHw*)

```
<!DOCTYPE html>
<html lang="en">
<body>

<a href="#">Hi</a>
```

```
<script>

var anchor = document.querySelector('a');

//element own properties
console.log(Object.keys(anchor).sort());

//element own properties and inherited properties
var documentPropertiesIncludeInherited = [];
for(var p in document){
    documentPropertiesIncludeInherited.push(p);
}
console.log(documentPropertiesIncludeInherited.sort());

//element inherited properties only
var documentPropertiesOnlyInherited = [];
for(var p in document){
    if(!document.hasOwnProperty(p)){
        documentPropertiesOnlyInherited.push(p);
    }
}
console.log(documentPropertiesOnlyInherited.sort());

</script>
</body>
</html>
```

Many properties are available, even if the inherited properties were not considered. Here is a list of noteworthy properties and methods (including inherited) that I handpicked for the context of this chapter:

- createElement()
- tagName
- children
- getAttribute()
- setAttribute()
- hasAttribute()
- removeAttribute()
- classList()
- dataset
- attributes

For a complete list, check out the MDN documentation (*http://mzl.la/YRmqp5*), which covers the general properties and methods available to most HTML elements.

3.3 Creating Elements

Element nodes are instantiated for us when a browser interprets an HTML document and a corresponding DOM is built based on the contents of the document. After this fact, it's also possible to programmatically create Element nodes using createEle ment(). In the following code, I create a <textarea> element node and then inject that node into the live DOM tree.

Live code (*http://jsfiddle.net/domenlightenment/d3Yvv*)

```
<!DOCTYPE html>
<html lang="en">
<body>
<script>

var elementNode = document.createElement('textarea'); /* HTMLTextAreaElement()
                                                  constructs <textarea> */
document.body.appendChild(elementNode);

console.log(document.querySelector('textarea')); //verify it's now in the DOM

</script>
</body>
</html>
```

The value passed to the createElement() method is a string that specifies the type of element [a.k.a. tagName (*http://bit.ly/14DnOfk*)] to be created.

Note
The value passed to createElement is changed to a lowercase string before the element is created.

3.4 Getting the Tag Name of an Element

Using the tagName property, we can access the name of an element. The tagName property returns the same value that using nodeName would return. Both return the value in uppercase, regardless of the case in the source HTML document.

In the following code, I get the name of an <a> element in the DOM.

Live code (*http://jsfiddle.net/domenlightenment/YJb3W*)

```
<!DOCTYPE html>
<html lang="en">
<body>

<a href="#">Hi</a>

<script>

console.log(document.querySelector('a').tagName); //logs A

//the nodeName property returns the same value
console.log(document.querySelector('a').nodeName); //logs A

</script>
</body>
</html>
```

3.5 Getting a List/Collection of Element Attributes and Values

Using the `attributes` property (inherited by element nodes from `Node`), we can get a collection of the `Attr` nodes (*http://bit.ly/14DpTrC*) that an element currently has defined. The list returned is a `NamedNodeMap` (*http://mzl.la/WDbKr8*). In the following code, I loop over the attributes collection, exposing each `Attr` node object contained in the collection.

Live code (*http://jsfiddle.net/domenlightenment/9gVQf*)

```
<!DOCTYPE html>
<html lang="en">
<body>

<a href='#' title="title" data-foo="dataFoo" class="yes" style="margin:0;"
   foo="boo"></a>

<script>

var atts = document.querySelector('a').attributes;

for(var i=0; i< atts.length; i++){
    console.log(atts[i].nodeName +'='+ atts[i].nodeValue);
}

</script>
</body>
</html>
```

Notes

The array returned from accessing the `attributes` property should be considered live. This means its contents can be changed at any time.

The array that is returned inherits from the `NamedNodeMap`, which provides methods to operate on the array, such as `getNamedItem()`, `setNamedItem()`, and `removeNamedItem()`. Operating on attributes with these methods should be secondary to using `getAttribute()`, `setAttribute()`, `hasAttribute()`, and `removeAttribute()`. It's this author's opinion that dealing with `Attr` nodes (*http://bit.ly/14DpTrC*) is messy. The only benefit in using `attributes` is found in its functionality for returning a list of live attributes.

The `attributes` property is an array-like collection and has a read-only `length` property.

Boolean attributes (e.g., `<option selected>foo</option>`) show up in the `attributes` list, but of course they have no value unless you provide one (e.g., `<option selected="selected">foo</option>`).

3.6 Getting, Setting, and Removing an Element's Attribute Value

The most consistent way to get, set, and remove an element's attribute (*http://bit.ly/14vbs8d*) value is to use the `getAttribute()`, `setAttribute()`, and `removeAttribute()` methods. In the following code, I demonstrate each method for managing element attributes.

Live code (*http://jsfiddle.net/domenlightenment/wp7rq*)

```
<!DOCTYPE html>
<html lang="en">
<body>

<a href='#' title="title" data-foo="dataFoo" style="margin:0;" class="yes"
  foo="boo" hidden="hidden">#link</a>

<script>

var atts = document.querySelector('a');

//remove attributes
atts.removeAttribute('href');
atts.removeAttribute('title');
atts.removeAttribute('style');
atts.removeAttribute('data-foo');
atts.removeAttribute('class');
atts.removeAttribute('foo'); //custom attribute
atts.removeAttribute('hidden'); //boolean attribute
```

```
//set (really re-set) attributes
atts.setAttribute('href','#');
atts.setAttribute('title','title');
atts.setAttribute('style','margin:0;');
atts.setAttribute('data-foo','dataFoo');
atts.setAttribute('class','yes');
atts.setAttribute('foo','boo');
atts.setAttribute('hidden','hidden'); /* boolean attribute requires sending the
                                         attribute as the value too */

//get attributes
console.log(atts.getAttribute('href'));
console.log(atts.getAttribute('title'));
console.log(atts.getAttribute('style'));
console.log(atts.getAttribute('data-foo'));
console.log(atts.getAttribute('class'));
console.log(atts.getAttribute('foo'));
console.log(atts.getAttribute('hidden'));

</script>
</body>
</html>
```

Notes

Use removeAttribute() instead of setting the attribute value to null or '' using setAttribute().

Some element attributes are available from element nodes as object properties (i.e., document.body.id or document.body.className). This author recommends avoiding these properties and using the remove, set, and get attribute methods.

3.7 Verifying Whether an Element Has a Specific Attribute

The best way to determine (i.e., true or false) whether an element has an attribute is to use the hasAttribute() method. In the following code, I verify whether the <a> has an href, title, style, data-foo, class, and foo attribute.

Live code (*http://jsfiddle.net/domenlightenment/hbCCE*)

```
<!DOCTYPE html>
<html lang="en">
<body>

<a href='#' title="title" data-foo="dataFoo" style="margin:0;" class="yes"
    goo></a>

<script>
```

```
var atts = document.querySelector('a');

console.log(
    atts.hasAttribute('href'),
    atts.hasAttribute('title'),
    atts.hasAttribute('style'),
    atts.hasAttribute('data-foo'),
    atts.hasAttribute('class'),
    atts.hasAttribute('goo') /* Notice this is true regardless of whether a value
                                is defined */
)

</script>
</body>
</html>
```

This method will return true if the element contains the attribute, even if the attribute has no value. For example, using hasAttribute(), we can get a Boolean response for Boolean attributes (*http://bit.ly/VsPTPP*). In the code example that follows, I test to see whether a checkbox is checked.

Live code (*http://jsfiddle.net/domenlightenment/tb6Ja*)

```
<!DOCTYPE html>
<html lang="en">
<body>

<input type="checkbox" checked></input>

<script>

var atts = document.querySelector('input');

console.log(atts.hasAttribute('checked')); //logs true

</script>
</body>
</html>
```

3.8 Getting a List of Class Attribute Values

Using the classList property available on element nodes, we can access a list [i.e., DOMTokenList (*http://bit.ly/VzGviA*)] of class attribute values that is much easier to work with than a space-delimited string value returned from the className property. In the following code, I contrast the use of classList with className.

Live code (*http://jsfiddle.net/domenlightenment/DLJEA*)

```
<!DOCTYPE html>
<html lang="en">
```

```
<body>

<div class="big brown bear"></div>

<script>

var elm = document.querySelector('div');

console.log(elm.classList); /* big brown bear {0="big", 1="brown",
                               2="bear", length=3, ...} */
console.log(elm.className); //logs 'big brown bear'

</script>
</body>
</html>
```

Notes

Given that the classList is an array-like collection, it has a read-only length property.

classList is read-only but can be modified using the add(), re move(), contains(), and toggle() methods.

IE 9 does not support classList. Support will be available in IE 10 (*http://bit.ly/12fn4xk*). Several polyfills are available (such as *https:// github.com/eligrey/classList.js* or *https://gist.github.com/1381839*).

3.9 Adding and Removing Subvalues to a Class Attribute

Using the classList.add() and classList.remove() methods, it's extremely simple to edit the value of a class attribute. In the following code, I demonstrate adding and removing class values.

Live code (*http://jsfiddle.net/domenlightenment/YVaUU*)

```
<!DOCTYPE html>
<html lang="en">
<body>
<div class="dog"></div>

<script>

var elm = document.querySelector('div');

elm.classList.add('cat');
elm.classList.remove('dog');
console.log(elm.className); //'cat'

</script>
```

```
</body>
</html>
```

3.10 Toggling a Class Attribute Value

Using the `classList.toggle()` method, we can toggle a subvalue of the class attribute. This allows us to add a value if it's missing or remove a value if it has already been added. In the following code, I toggle the `'visible'` value and the `'grow'` value. This essentially means I remove `'visible'` and add `'grow'` to the class attribute value.

Live code (*http://jsfiddle.net/domenlightenment/uFp6J*)

```
<!DOCTYPE html>
<html lang="en">
<body>
<div class="visible"></div>

<script>

var elm = document.querySelector('div');

elm.classList.toggle('visible');
elm.classList.toggle('grow');
console.log(elm.className); //'grow'

</script>
</body>
</html>
```

3.11 Determining Whether a Class Attribute Value Contains a Specific Value

Using the `classList.contains()` method, it's possible to determine (i.e., true or false) whether a class attribute value contains a specific subvalue. In the following code, I test whether the `<div>` class attribute contains a subvalue of `brown`.

Live code (*http://jsfiddle.net/domenlightenment/njyaP*)

```
<!DOCTYPE html>
<html lang="en">
<body>
<div class="big brown bear"></div>

<script>

var elm = document.querySelector('div');

console.log(elm.classList.contains('brown')); //logs true
```

```
</script>
</body>
</html>
```

3.12 Getting and Setting data-* Attributes

The dataset property of an element node provides an object containing all the attributes of an element that start with data-*. Because it's simply a JavaScript object, we can manipulate dataset and have the element in the DOM reflect those changes.

Live code (*http://jsfiddle.net/domenlightenment/ystgj*)

```
<!DOCTYPE html>
<html lang="en">
<body>

<div data-foo-foo="foo" data-bar-bar="bar"></div>

<script>

var elm = document.querySelector('div');

//get
console.log(elm.dataset.fooFoo); //logs 'foo'
console.log(elm.dataset.barBar); //logs 'bar'

//set
elm.dataset.gooGoo = 'goo';
console.log(elm.dataset); /* logs DOMStringMap {fooFoo="foo", barBar="bar",
                             gooGoo="goo"} */

//what the element looks like in the DOM
console.log(elm); /* logs <div data-foo-foo="foo" data-bar-bar="bar"
                    data-goo-goo="goo"> */

</script>
</body>
</html>
```

Notes

dataset contains camelCase versions of data attributes. This means data-foo-foo will be listed as the property fooFoo in the dataset DOM StringMap object. The hyphen is replaced by camelCasing.

Removing a data-* attribute from the DOM is as simple as using the delete operator on a property of the dataset (e.g., delete data set.fooFoo).

dataset is not supported in IE 9. A polyfill (*http://bit.ly/YoKOKP*) is available.

However, you can always just use getAttribute('data-foo'), removeAttribute('data-foo'), setAttribute('data-foo'), and hasAttribute('data-foo').

CHAPTER 4

Element Node Selection

4.1 Selecting a Specific Element Node

The most common methods for getting a reference to a single element node are:

- querySelector()
- getElementById()

In the following code, I leverage both of these methods to select an element node from the HTML document.

Live code (*http://jsfiddle.net/domenlightenment/b4Rch*)

```
<!DOCTYPE html>
<html lang="en">
<body>

<ul>
<li>Hello</li>
<li>big</li>
<li>bad</li>
<li id="last">world</li>
</ul>

<script>

console.log(document.querySelector('li').textContent); //logs Hello
console.log(document.getElementById('last').textContent); //logs world

</script>
</body>
</html>
```

The getElementById() method is pretty simple compared to the more robust query
Selector() method. The querySelector() method permits a parameter in the form
of a CSS selector syntax (*http://www.w3.org/TR/css3-selectors/#selectors*). Basically, you
can pass this method a CSS3 selector (e.g., #score>tbody>tr>td:nth-of-type(2)),
which it will use to select a single element in the DOM.

Notes

querySelector() will return the first node element found in the document based on the selector. For example, in the preceding code, I pass
a selector that will select all the <li> elements in CSS, but only the first
one is returned.

querySelector() is also defined on element nodes. This allows the
method to limit its results to a specific vein of the DOM tree, thereby
enabling context quering.

4.2 Selecting/Creating a List (a.k.a. NodeList) of Element Nodes

The most common methods for selecting/creating a list of nodes in an HTML document
are:

- querySelectorAll()
- getElementsByTagName()
- getElementsByClassName()

In the following code, I use all three of these methods to create a list of the <li> elements
in the document.

Live code (*http://jsfiddle.net/domenlightenment/nT7Lr*)

```
<!DOCTYPE html>
<html lang="en">
<body>

<ul>
<li class="liClass">Hello</li>
<li class="liClass">big</li>
<li class="liClass">bad</li>
<li class="liClass">world</li>
</ul>

<script>
```

```
/* all of the methods below create/select the same list of <li> elements from
the DOM */
console.log(document.querySelectorAll('li'));
console.log(document.getElementsByTagName('li'));
console.log(document.getElementsByClassName('liClass'));

</script>
</body>
</html>
```

Note that the methods used in the preceding code example do not select a specific element; instead, they create a list of elements [a NodeList (*http://mzl.la/14Dr5eO*)] from which you can choose.

Notes

NodeLists created from getElementsByTagName() and getElements ByClassName() are considered live and will always reflect the state of the document, even if the document is updated after the list is created/ selected.

The querySelectorAll() method does not return a live list of elements. This means the list created from querySelectorAll() is a snapshot of the document at the time it was created and does not reflect the document as it changes. The list is static, not live.

querySelectorAll(), getElementsByTagName(), and getElementsBy ClassName are also defined on element nodes. This allows the methods to limit their results to a specific vein (or set of veins) of the DOM tree (e.g., document.getElementById('header').getElementsByClass Name('a')).

I did not mention the getElementsByName() method, as it does not commonly leverage over other solutions, but you should be aware of its existence for selecting from a document form, img, frame, embed, and object elements that all have the same name attribute value.

Passing either querySelectorAll() or getElementsByTagName() the string '*', which generally means "all," will return a list of all elements in the document.

Keep in mind that childNodes will also return a NodeList, just like querySelectorAll(), getElementsByTagName(), and getElementsBy ClassName.

The NodeLists are array-like lists/collections and have a read-only length property (but they do not inherit array methods).

4.3 Selecting All Immediate Child Element Nodes

Using the `children` property from an element node, we can get a list [an HTMLCollection (*https://developer.mozilla.org/en/DOM/HTMLCollection*)] of all the immediate child nodes that are element nodes. In the following code, I use `children` to create a selection/list of all the `<li>`s contained within the `<ul>`.

Live code (*http://jsfiddle.net/domenlightenment/svfRC*)

```
<!DOCTYPE html>
<html lang="en">
<body>

<ul>
<li><strong>Hi</strong></li>
<li>there</li>
</ul>

<script>

var ulElement = document.querySelector('ul').children;

//logs a list/array of all immediate child element nodes
console.log(ulElement); //logs [<li>, <li>]

</script>
</body>
</html>
```

Notice that using `children` only gives us the immediate element nodes, excluding any nodes (e.g., text nodes) that are not elements. If the element has no children, `children` will return an empty array-like list.

Notes

HTMLCollections contain elements in document order; that is, they are placed in the array in the order the elements appear in the DOM.

HTMLCollections are live, which means any change to the document will be reflected dynamically in the collection.

4.4 Selecting Contextual Elements

The methods `querySelector()`, `querySelectorAll()`, `getElementsByTagName()`, and `getElementsByClassName`, typically accessed from the `document` object, are also defined on element nodes. This allows these methods to limit their results to a specific vein (or set of veins) of the DOM tree. In other words, you can select a specific context in which you would like the methods to search for element nodes by invoking these methods on element node objects.

Live code (*http://jsfiddle.net/domenlightenment/fL6tV*)

```html
<!DOCTYPE html>
<html lang="en">
<body>

<div>
<ul>
<li class="liClass">Hello</li>
<li class="liClass">big</li>
<li class="liClass">bad</li>
<li class="liClass">world</li>
</ul>
</div>

<ul>
<li class="liClass">Hello</li>
</ul>

<script>

/* select a div as the context to run the selecting methods only on the
contents of the div */
var div = document.querySelector('div');

console.log(div.querySelector('ul'));
console.log(div.querySelectorAll('li'));
console.log(div.getElementsByTagName('li'));
console.log(div.getElementsByClassName('liClass'));

</script>
</body>
</html>
```

These methods operate not only on the live DOM, but also on programmatic DOM structures that are created in code.

Live code (*http://jsfiddle.net/domenlightenment/CCnva*)

```html
<!DOCTYPE html>
<html lang="en">
<body>

<script>
//create DOM structure
var divElm = document.createElement('div');
var ulElm = document.createElement('ul');
var liElm = document.createElement('li');
liElm.setAttribute('class','liClass');
ulElm.appendChild(liElm);
```

```
divElm.appendChild(ulElm);

//use selecting methods on DOM structure
console.log(divElm.querySelector('ul'));
console.log(divElm.querySelectorAll('li'));
console.log(divElm.getElementsByTagName('li'));
console.log(divElm.getElementsByClassName('liClass'));

</body>
</html>
```

4.5 Preconfigured Selections/Lists of Element Nodes

You should be aware that there are some preconfigured, legacy array-like lists, containing element nodes from an HTML document. In the following list, I cover a few of these that might be handy to be aware of:

document.all
> All elements in the HTML document

document.forms
> All <form> elements in the HTML document

document.images
> All <img> elements in the HTML document

document.links
> All <a> elements in the HTML document

document.scripts
> All <script> elements in the HTML document

document.styleSheets
> All <link> or <style> elements in the HTML document

Notes

These preconfigured arrays are constructed from the HTMLCollec tion interface/object (*http://mzl.la/VsQCAn*), except for docu ment.styleSheets, which uses StyleSheetList.

HTMLCollection (*http://mzl.la/11degsA*) is live, just like NodeList (*http://mzl.la/14Dr5eO*) [except for querySelectorAll()].

Oddly, document.all is constructed from an HTMLAllCollection, not an HTMLCollection, and is not supported in Firefox.

4.6 Using matchesSelector() to Verify That an Element Will Be Selected

Using the `matchesSelector()` method, we can determine whether an element will match a selector string. For example, say we want to determine whether an `<li>` is the first child element of a `<ul>`. In the following code example, I select the first `<li>` inside the `<ul>` and then ask whether that element matches the selector, `li:first-child`. Because if it in fact does, the `matchesSelector()` method returns `true`.

Live code (*http://jsfiddle.net/domenlightenment/9RayM*)

```
<!DOCTYPE html>
<html lang="en">
<body>

<ul>
<li>Hello</li>
<li>world</li>
</ul>

<script>

//fails in modern browser must use browser prefix moz, webkit, o, and ms
console.log(document.querySelector('li').matchesSelector('li:first-child'));
//logs false

//prefix moz
/* console.log(document.querySelector('li').mozMatchesSelector
('li:first-child')); */

//prefix webkit
/* console.log(document.querySelector('li').webkitMatchesSelector
('li:first-child')); */

//prefix o
/* console.log(document.querySelector('li').oMatchesSelector
('li:first-child')); */

//prefix ms
/* console.log(document.querySelector('li').msMatchesSelector
('li:first-child')); */

</script>
</body>
</html>
```

Notes

matchesSelector() has not seen much love from the browsers, as its usage is behind that of the browser prefixes mozMatchesSelector(), webkitMatchesSelector(), oMatchesSelector(), and msMatchesSe lector().

In the future, matchesSelector() will be renamed to matches().

CHAPTER 5

Element Node Geometry and Scrolling Geometry

5.1 Element Node Size, Offsets, and Scrolling Overview

DOM nodes are parsed and painted (*http://www.html5rocks.com/en/tutorials/inter nals/howbrowserswork/#Painting*) into visual shapes when viewing HTML documents in a web browser. Nodes, mostly element nodes, have a corresponding visual representation made viewable/visual by browsers. To inspect and in some cases manipulate the visual representation and geometry of nodes programmatically, a set of APIs exist and are specified in the CSSOM View Module (*http://www.w3.org/TR/cssom-view/*). A subset of methods and properties found in this specification provide an API to determine the geometry (i.e., size and position using offset) of element nodes as well as hooks for manipulating scrollable nodes and getting values of scrolled nodes. This chapter breaks down these methods and properties.

Note

Most of the properties (excluding `scrollLeft` and `scrollTop`) from the CSSOM View Module specification are read-only and calculated each time they are accessed. In other words, the values are live.

5.2 Getting an Element's offsetTop and offsetLeft Values Relative to the offsetParent

Using the properties `offsetTop` and `offsetLeft`, we can get the offset pixel value of an element node from the `offsetParent`. These element node properties give us the distance in pixels from an element's outside top and left borders to the inside top and left borders of the `offsetParent`. The value of the `offsetParent` is determined by searching the nearest ancestor elements for an element that has a CSS position value not equal to static. If none are found, the <body> element, or what some refer to as the "document" (as opposed to the browser viewport), is the offsetParent value. If, during the ancestral search, a <td>, <th>, or <table> element with a CSS position value of static is found, this becomes the value of offsetParent.

Let's verify that offsetTop and offsetLeft provide the values one might expect. The properties offsetLeft and offsetTop in the following code tell us that the <div> with an id of red is 60 pixels from the top and left of the offsetParent (i.e., the <body> element in this example).

Live code (*http://jsfiddle.net/domenlightenment/dj5h9*)

```
<!DOCTYPE html>
<html lang="en">
<head>
<style>
body{margin:0;}
#blue{height:100px;width:100px;background-color:blue;border:10px solid gray;
  padding:25px;margin:25px;}
#red{height:50px;width:50px;background-color:red;border:10px solid gray;}
</style>
</head>
<body>

<div id="blue"><div id="red"></div></div>

<script>

var div = document.querySelector('#red');

console.log(div.offsetLeft); //logs 60
console.log(div.offsetTop); //logs 60
console.log(div.offsetParent); //logs <body>

</script>
</body>
</html>
```

Take a look at Figure 5-1, which shows what the code displays in the browser, to get a better understanding of how the offsetLeft and offsetTop values are determined. The red <div> shown in the image is exactly 60 pixels from the offsetParent.

Notice that I am measuring from the outside border of the red <div> element to the inside border of the offsetParent (i.e., the <body>).

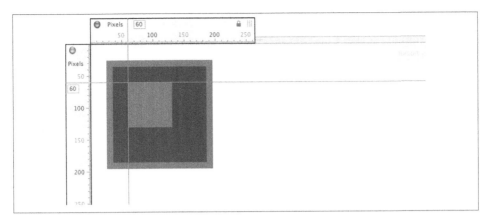

Figure 5-1. <div id="red"></div> is 60 pixels from offsetParent

As I mentioned previously, if I were to change the blue <div> in the preceding code to have a position of absolute, this would alter the value of the offsetParent. In the following code, absolutely positioning the blue <div> will cause the values returned from offsetLeft and offsetTop to report an offset of 25 pixels. This is because the offset parent is now the blue <div> and not the <body>.

Live code (*http://jsfiddle.net/domenlightenment/ft2ZQ*)

```
<!DOCTYPE html>
<html lang="en">
<head>
<style>
#blue{height:100px;width:100px;background-color:blue;border:10px solid gray;
   padding:25px;margin:25px;position:absolute;}
#red{height:50px;width:50px;background-color:red;border:10px solid gray;}
</style>
</head>
<body>

<div id="blue"><div id="red"></div></div>

<script>

var div = document.querySelector('#red');

console.log(div.offsetLeft); //logs 25
console.log(div.offsetTop); //logs 25
console.log(div.offsetParent); //logs <div id="blue">

</script>
</body>
</html>
```

The image of the browser view shown in Figure 5-2 clarifies the new measurements returned from offsetLeft and offsetTop when the offsetParent is the blue <div>.

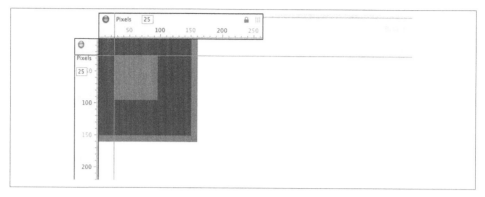

Figure 5-2. <div id="red"></div> is 25 pixels from offsetParent

 Notes

Many of the browsers break the outside border to the inside border measurement when the offsetParent is the <body> and the <body> or <html> element has a visible margin, padding, or border value.

offsetParent, offsetTop, and offsetLeft are extensions to the HTMLElement object.

5.3 Using getBoundingClientRect() to Get an Element's Top, Right, Bottom, and Left Border Edge Offsets Relative to the Viewport

Using the getBoundingClientRect() method, we can get the position of an element's outside border edges as the element is painted in the browser viewport relative to the top and left edges of the viewport. This means the left and right edges are measured from the outside border edge of an element to the left edge of the viewport, and the top and bottom edges are measured from the outside border edge of an element to the top edge of the viewport.

In the following code, I create a 50 × 50-pixel <div> with a 10-pixel border and a 100-pixel margin. To get the distance in pixels from each border edge of the <div>, I call the getBoundingClientRect() method on the <div>, which returns an object containing a top, right, bottom, and left property.

```
<!DOCTYPE html>
<html lang="en">
<head>
<style>
body{margin:0;}
div{height:50px;width:50px;background-color:red;border:10px solid gray;
  margin:100px;}
</style>
</head>
<body>

<div></div>

<script>

var divEdges = document.querySelector('div').getBoundingClientRect();

console.log(divEdges.top, divEdges.right, divEdges.bottom, divEdges.left);
//logs '100 170 170 100'

</script>
</body>
</html>
```

Figure 5-3 shows the browser-rendered view of the preceding code with some added measurement indicators to show exactly how getBoundingClientRect() is calculated.

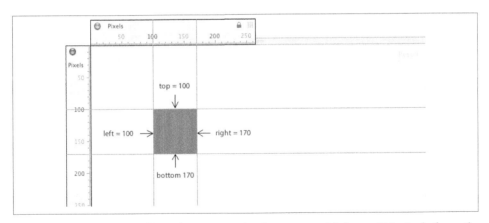

Figure 5-3. <div id="red"></div> top, right, bottom, and left are 100 pixels from the viewport edge

The top outside border edge of the <div> element is 100 pixels from the top edge of the viewport. The right outside border edge of the <div> element is 170 pixels from the left edge of the viewport. The bottom outside border edge of the <div> element is 170 pixels from the top edge of the viewport. And the left outside border edge of the <div> element is 100 pixels from the left edge of the viewport.

5.4 Getting an Element's Size (Border + Padding + Content) in the Viewport

The getBoundingClientRect() method returns an object with a top, right, bottom, and left property/value as well as a height and width property/value. The height and width properties indicate the size of the element where the total size is derived by adding together the content of the div, its padding, and its borders.

In the following code, I use getBoundingClientRect() to get the size of the <div> element in the DOM.

Live code (*http://jsfiddle.net/domenlightenment/PuXmL*)

```
<!DOCTYPE html>
<html lang="en">
<head>
<style>
div{height:25px;width:25px;background-color:red;border:25px solid gray;
  padding:25px;}
</style>
</head>
<body>

<div></div>

<script>

var div = document.querySelector('div').getBoundingClientRect();

console.log(div.height, div.width); //logs '125 125'
//because 25px border + 25px padding + 25 content + 25 padding + 25 border = 125

</script>
</body>
</html>
```

The same size values can also be found using the offsetHeight and offsetWidth properties. In the following code, I leverage these properties to get the same height and width values provided by getBoundingClientRect().

Live code (*http://jsfiddle.net/domenlightenment/MSzL3*)

```
<!DOCTYPE html>
<html lang="en">
<head>
```

```
<style>
div{height:25px;width:25px;background-color:red;border:25px solid gray;
  padding:25px;}
</style>
</head>
<body>

<div></div>

<script>

var div = document.querySelector('div');

console.log(div.offsetHeight, div.offsetWidth); //logs '125 125'
//because 25px border + 25px padding + 25 content + 25 padding + 25 border = 125

</script>
</body>
</html>
```

5.5 Getting an Element's Size (Padding + Content) in the Viewport, Excluding Borders

The clientWidth and clientHeight properties return the total size of an element by adding together the content of the element and its padding, excluding the border sizes. In the following code, I use these two properties to get the height and width of an element, including padding but excluding borders.

Live code (*http://jsfiddle.net/domenlightenment/bSrSb*)

```
<!DOCTYPE html>
<html lang="en">
<head>
<style>
div{height:25px;width:25px;background-color:red;border:25px solid gray;
  padding:25px;}
</style>
</head>
<body>

<div></div>

<script>

var div = document.querySelector('div');

console.log(div.clientHeight, div.clientWidth); /* logs '75 75' because
                                   25px padding + 25 content +
                                   25 padding = 75 */
```

```
</script>
</body>
</html>
```

5.6 Using elementFromPoint() to Get the Topmost Element in the Viewport at a Specific Point

Using elementFromPoint(), it's possible to get a reference to the topmost element in an HTML document at a specific point in the document. In the following code example, I simply ask what is the topmost element 50 pixels from the top and left of the viewport. Since we have two <div>s at that location, the topmost div (or, if there is no z-index set, the last one in document order) is selected and returned.

Live code (*http://jsfiddle.net/domenlightenment/8ksS5*)

```
<!DOCTYPE html>
<html lang="en">
<head>
<style>
div{height:50px;width:50px;background-color:red;position:absolute;top:50px;
  left:50px;}
</style>
</head>
<body>

<div id="bottom"></div><div id="top"></div>

<script>

console.log(document.elementFromPoint(50,50)); //logs <div id="top">

</script>
</body>
</html>
```

5.7 Using scrollHeight and scrollWidth to Get the Size of the Element Being Scrolled

The scrollHeight and scrollWidth properties simply give you the height and width of the node being scrolled. For example, open any HTML document that scrolls in a web browser and access these properties on the <html> (e.g., document.documentEle ment.scrollWidth) or <body> (e.g., document.body.scrollWidth), and you will get the total size of the HTML document being scrolled. Since we can apply scrolling, using CSS (i.e., overflow:scroll), to elements, let's look at a simpler code example. In the following code, I make a <div> scroll a <p> element that is 1,000 × 1,000 pixels. Accessing the `scrollHeight` and `scrollWidth` properties on the `<div>` will tell us that the element being scrolled is 1,000 × 1,000 pixels.

Live code (*http://jsfiddle.net/domenlightenment/9sZtZ*)

```
<!DOCTYPE html>
<html lang="en">
<head>
<style>
*{margin:0;padding:0;}
div{height:100px;width:100px; overflow:auto;}
p{height:1000px;width:1000px;background-color:red;}
</style>
</head>
<body>

<div><p></p></div>

<script>

var div = document.querySelector('div');

console.log(div.scrollHeight, div.scrollWidth); //logs '1000 1000'

</script>
</body>
</html>
```

Note

If you need to know the height and width of the node inside a scrollable area when the node is smaller than the viewport of the scrollable area, don't use `scrollHeight` and `scrollWidth`, as they will give you the size of the viewport. If the node being scrolled is smaller than the scroll area, use `clientHeight` and `clientWidth` to determine the size of the node contained in the scrollable area.

5.8 Using scrollTop and scrollLeft to Get and Set Pixels Scrolled from the Top and Left

The `scrollTop` and `scrollLeft` properties are read/write properties that return the pixels to the left or top that are not currently viewable in the scrollable viewport due to scrolling. In the following code, I set up a `<div>` that scrolls a `<p>` element.

Live code (*http://jsfiddle.net/domenlightenment/DqZYH*)

```
<!DOCTYPE html>
<html lang="en">
<head>
```

```
<style>
div{height:100px;width:100px;overflow:auto;}
p{height:1000px;width:1000px;background-color:red;}
</style>
</head>
<body>

<div><p></p></div>

<script>

var div = document.querySelector('div');

div.scrollTop = 750;
div.scrollLeft = 750;

console.log(div.scrollTop,div.scrollLeft); //logs '750 750'

</script>
</body>
</html>
```

I programmatically scroll the <div> by setting scrollTop and scrollLeft to 750. Then I get the current value of scrollTop and scrollLeft, which, since we just set the value to 750, will return a value of 750. The 750 reports the number of pixels scrolled and indicates 750 pixels to the left and top are not viewable in the viewport. If it helps, just think of these properties as the pixel measurements of the content that is not shown in the viewport to the left or top.

5.9 Using scrollIntoView() to Scroll an Element into View

By selecting a node contained inside a node that is scrollable, we can tell the selected node to scroll into view by using the scrollIntoView() method. In the following code, I select the fifth <p> element contained in the scrolling <div> and call scrollInto View() on it.

Live code (*http://jsfiddle.net/domenlightenment/SyeFZ*)

```
<!DOCTYPE html>
<html lang="en">
<head>
<style>
div{height:30px;width:30px; overflow:auto;}
p{background-color:red;}
</style>
</head>
<body>
```

```
<div>
<content>
<p>1</p>
<p>2</p>
<p>3</p>
<p>4</p>
<p>5</p>
<p>6</p>
<p>7</p>
<p>8</p>
<p>9</p>
<p>10</p>
</content>
</div>

<script>

/* select <p>5</p> and scroll that element into view, I pass children '4' because
it's a zero index array-like structure */
document.querySelector('content').children[4].scrollIntoView(true);

</script>
</body>
</html>
```

By passing the scrollIntoView() method a parameter of true, I am telling the method to scroll to the top of the element being scrolled to. The true parameter is not needed, however, as this is the default action performed by the method. If you want to scroll to the bottom of the element, pass a parameter of false to the scrollIntoView() method.

Element Node Inline Styles

6.1 Style Attribute (a.k.a. Element Inline CSS Properties) Overview

Every HTML element has a style attribute that can be used to insert inline CSS properties specific to the element. In the following code, I am accessing the style attribute of a <div> that contains several inline CSS properties.

Live code (*http://jsfiddle.net/domenlightenment/A4Aph*)

```
<!DOCTYPE html>
<html lang="en">
<body>

<div style="background-color:red;border:1px solid black;height:100px;
  width:100px;"></div>

<script>

var divStyle = document.querySelector('div').style;

//logs CSSStyleDeclaration {0="background-color", ...}
console.log(divStyle);

  </script>
</body>
</html>
```

Notice in the code that the style property returns a CSSStyleDeclaration object and not a string. Additionally, note that only the element's inline styles (i.e., not the computed styles, which are any styles that have cascaded from stylesheets) are included in the CSSStyleDeclaration object.

6.2 Getting, Setting, and Removing Individual Inline CSS Properties

Inline CSS styles are individually represented as a property (i.e., an object property) of the style object available on element node objects. This provides the interface for us to get, set, or remove individual CSS properties on an element by simply setting an object's property value. In the following code, I set, get, and remove styles on a <div> by manipulating the properties of the style object.

Live code (*http://jsfiddle.net/domenlightenment/xNT85*)

```
<!DOCTYPE html>
<html lang="en">
<body>

<div></div>

<script>

var divStyle = document.querySelector('div').style;

//set
divStyle.backgroundColor = 'red';
divStyle.border = '1px solid black';
divStyle.width = '100px';
divStyle.height = '100px';

//get
console.log(divStyle.backgroundColor);
console.log(divStyle.border);
console.log(divStyle.width);
console.log(divStyle.height);

/* remove
divStyle.backgroundColor = '';
divStyle.border = '';
divStyle.width = '';
divStyle.height = '';
*/

</script>
</body>
</html>
```

Notes

The property names contained in the `style` object do not contain the normal hyphen that is used in CSS property names. The translation is pretty simple. Remove the hyphen and use camelCase (e.g., `font-size` = `fontSize` and `background-image` = `backgroundImage`). In the case in which a CSS property name is a JavaScript keyword, the JavaScript CSS property name is prefixed with `css` (e.g., `float` = `cssFloat`).

Shorthand properties are available as properties as well. So you can set `margin` as well as `marginTop`.

For any CSS property value that requires a unit of measure, remember to include the appropriate unit (e.g., `style.width` = `'300px'`; not `style.width` = `'300'`;). When a document is rendered in standards mode, the unit of measure is required; otherwise, it will be ignored. In quirks mode, assumptions are made if no unit of measure is included.

Table 6-1 lists some CSS properties and their equivalents in JavaScript.

Table 6-1. CSS properties translated to JavaScript property names

CSS property	JavaScript property
background	background
background-attachment	backgroundAttachment
background-color	backgroundColor
background-image	backgroundImage
background-position	backgroundPosition
background-repeat	backgroundRepeat
border	border
border-bottom	borderBottom
border-bottom-color	borderBottomColor
border-bottom-style	borderBottomStyle
border-bottom-width	borderBottomWidth
border-color	borderColor
border-left	borderLeft
border-left-color	borderLeftColor
border-left-style	borderLeftStyle
border-left-width	borderLeftWidth
border-right	borderRight
border-right-color	borderRightColor
border-right-style	borderRightStyle

CSS property	JavaScript property
border-right-width	borderRightWidth
border-style	borderStyle
border-top	borderTop
border-top-color	borderTopColor
border-top-style	borderTopStyle
border-top-width	borderTopWidth
border-width	borderWidth
clear	clear
clip	clip
color	color
cursor	cursor
display	display
filter	filter
font	font
font-family	fontFamily
font-size	fontSize
font-variant	fontVariant
font-weight	fontWeight
height	height
left	left
letter-spacing	letterSpacing
line-height	lineHeight
list-style	listStyle
list-style-image	listStyleImage
list-style-position	listStylePosition
list-style-type	listStyleType
margin	margin
margin-bottom	marginBottom
margin-left	marginLeft
margin-right	marginRight
margin-top	marginTop
overflow	overflow
padding	padding
padding-bottom	paddingBottom
padding-left	paddingLeft

CSS property	JavaScript property
padding-right	paddingRight
padding-top	paddingTop
page-break-after	pageBreakAfter
page-break-before	pageBreakBefore
position	position
float	styleFloat
text-align	textAlign
text-decoration	textDecoration
text-decoration: blink	textDecorationBlink
text-decoration: line-through	textDecorationLineThrough
text-decoration: none	textDecorationNone
text-decoration: overline	textDecorationOverline
text-decoration: underline	textDecorationUnderline
text-indent	textIndent
text-transform	textTransform
top	top
vertical-align	verticalAlign
visibility	visibility
width	width
z-index	zIndex

The `style` object is a `CSSStyleDeclaration` object and it provides access not only to individual CSS properties, but also to the `setPropertyValue(propertyName)`, `get PropertyValue(propertyName,value)`, and `removeProperty()` methods used to manipulate individual CSS properties on an element node. In the following code, I set, get, and remove individual CSS properties on a `<div>` using these methods.

Live code (*http://jsfiddle.net/domenlightenment/X2DyX*)

```
<!DOCTYPE html>
<html lang="en">
<head>
<style>
</style>
</head>

<body>

<div style="background-color:green;border:1px solid purple;"

<script>
```

```
var divStyle = document.querySelector('div').style;

//set
divStyle.setProperty('background-color','red');
divStyle.setProperty('border','1px solid black');
divStyle.setProperty('width','100px');
divStyle.setProperty('height','100px');

//get
console.log(divStyle.getPropertyValue('background-color'));
console.log(divStyle.getPropertyValue('border'));
console.log(divStyle.getPropertyValue('width'));
console.log(divStyle.getPropertyValue('height'));

/* remove
divStyle.removeProperty('background-color');
divStyle.removeProperty('border');
divStyle.removeProperty('width');
divStyle.removeProperty('height');
*/

</script>
</body>
</html>
```

Note

The property name is passed to the setProperty() and getProperty Value() methods using the CSS property name plus a hyphen (e.g., background-color and not backgroundColor).

For more detailed information about the setProperty(), getProper tyValue(), and removeProperty() methods, as well as additional properties and methods, consult the Mozilla documentation (*https:// developer.mozilla.org/en/DOM/CSSStyleDeclaration*).

6.3 Getting, Setting, and Removing All Inline CSS Properties

Using the cssText property of the CSSStyleDeclaration object, as well as the get Attribute() and setAttribute() methods, it's possible to get, set, and remove the entire value (i.e., all inline CSS properties) of the style attribute using a JavaScript string. In the following code, I get, set, and remove all inline CSS (as opposed to individually changing CSS properties) on a <div>.

```
<!DOCTYPE html>
<html lang="en">
<body>

<div></div>

<script>

var div = document.querySelector('div');
var divStyle = div.style;

//set using cssText
divStyle.cssText = 'background-color:red;border:1px solid black;height:100px;
  width:100px;';
//get using cssText
console.log(divStyle.cssText);
//remove
divStyle.cssText = '';

//exactly that same outcome using setAttribute() and getAttribute()

//set using setAttribute
div.setAttribute('style','background-color:red;border:1px solid black;
  height:100px;width:100px;');
//get using getAttribute
console.log(div.getAttribute('style'));
//remove
div.removeAttribute('style');

</script>
</body>
</html>
```

Note

Replacing the style attribute value with a new string is the fastest way to make multiple changes to an element's style.

6.4 Using getComputedStyle() to Get an Element's Computed Styles (i.e., Actual Styles Including Any from the Cascade)

The style property only contains the CSS that is defined via the style attribute. To get an element's CSS from the cascade (i.e., cascading from inline stylesheets, external stylesheets, and browser stylesheets) as well as its inline styles, you can use getCompu tedStyle(). This method provides a read-only CSSStyleDeclaration object similar to style. In the following code, I demonstrate the reading of cascading styles, not just element inline styles.

Live code (*http://jsfiddle.net/domenlightenment/k3G5Q*)

```html
<!DOCTYPE html>
<html lang="en">
<head>
<style>
 div{
    background-color:red;
    border:1px solid black;
    height:100px;
    width:100px;
}
</style>
</head>

<body>

<div style="background-color:green;border:1px solid purple;"></div>

<script>

var div = document.querySelector('div');

//logs rgb(0, 128, 0) or green, this is an inline element style
console.log(window.getComputedStyle(div).backgroundColor);

/* logs 1px solid rgb(128, 0, 128) or 1px solid purple, this is an inline
element style */
console.log(window.getComputedStyle(div).border);

//logs 100px, note this is not an inline element style
console.log(window.getComputedStyle(div).height);

//logs 100px, note this is not an inline element style
console.log(window.getComputedStyle(div).width);

</script>
</body>
</html>
```

The getComputedStyle() method honors the CSS specificity hierarchy (*http://css-tricks.com/specifics-on-css-specificity/*). For example, in the preceding code, the backgroundColor of the <div> is reported as green, not red, because inline styles are at the top of the specificity hierarchy; thus, the browser applies the inline backgroundColor value to the element and considers it to be the final computed style.

Notes

No values can be set on a CSSStyleDeclaration object returned from getComputedStyles(), as it's read-only.

The getComputedStyles() method returns color values in the rgb(#,#,#) format, regardless of how they were originally authored.

Shorthand properties (*http://bit.ly/YoM0Oc*) are not computed for the CSSStyleDeclaration object; you will have to use nonshorthand property names for property access (e.g., marginTop, not margin).

6.5 Using the class and id Attributes to Apply and Remove CSS Properties on an Element

Style rules defined in an inline stylesheet or an external stylesheet can be added or removed from an element by using the class and id attributes. This is the most common pattern for manipulating element styles. In the following code, leveraging setAttribute() and classList.add(), inline style rules are applied to a <div> by setting the class and id attribute values. Using removeAttribute() and classList.remove(), these CSS rules can be removed as well.

Live code (*http://jsfiddle.net/domenlightenment/BF9gM*)

```
<!DOCTYPE html>
<html lang="en">
<head>
<style>
.foo{
  background-color:red;
  padding:10px;
}
#bar{
  border:10px solid #000;
  margin:10px;
}
</style>
</head>
<body>

<div></div>

<script>

var div = document.querySelector('div');

//set
div.setAttribute('id','bar');
div.classList.add('foo');
```

```
/* remove
div.removeAttribute('id');
div.classList.remove('foo');
*/

</script>
</body>
</html>
```

Text Nodes

7.1 Text Object Overview

Text in an HTML document is represented by instances of the Text() constructor function, which produces text nodes. When an HTML document is parsed, the text mixed in among the elements of an HTML page is converted to text nodes.

Live code (*http://jsfiddle.net/domenlightenment/kuz5Z*)

```
<!DOCTYPE html>
<html lang="en">
<body>

<p>hi</p>

<script>
//select 'hi' text node
var textHi = document.querySelector('p').firstChild

console.log(textHi.constructor); //logs Text()

//logs Text {textContent="hi", length=2, wholeText="hi", ...}
console.log(textHi);

</script>
</body>
</html>
```

The preceding code concludes that the Text() constructor function constructs the text node, but keep in mind that Text inherits from CharacterData, Node, and Object.

7.2 Text Object and Properties

To get accurate information pertaining to the available properties and methods on a Text node, it's best to ignore the specification and to ask the browser what is available. Examine the arrays created in the following code detailing the properties and methods available from a text node.

Live code (*http://jsfiddle.net/domenlightenment/Wj3uS*)

```
<!DOCTYPE html>
<html lang="en">
<body>

<p>hi</p>

<script>
var text = document.querySelector('p').firstChild;

//text own properties
console.log(Object.keys(text).sort());

//text own properties and inherited properties
var textPropertiesIncludeInherited = [];
for(var p in text){
    textPropertiesIncludeInherited.push(p);
}
console.log(textPropertiesIncludeInherited.sort());

//text inherited properties only
var textPropertiesOnlyInherited = [];
for(var p in text){
    if(!text.hasOwnProperty(p)){
        textPropertiesOnlyInherited.push(p);
    }
}
console.log(textPropertiesOnlyInherited.sort());

</script>
</body>
</html>
```

Many properties are available, even if the inherited properties were not considered. The following properties and methods are noteworthy based on the context of this chapter:

- textContent
- splitText()
- appendData()
- deleteData()
- insertData()

- `replaceData()`
- `subStringData()`
- `normalize()`
- `data`
- `document.createTextNode()` (not a property or inherited property of text nodes but discussed in this chapter)

7.3 Whitespace Creates Text Nodes

When a DOM is constructed either by the browser or by programmatic means, text nodes are created from whitespace as well as from text characters. After all, whitespace is a character. In the following code, the second paragraph, containing an empty space, has a child text node while the first paragraph does not.

Live code (*http://jsfiddle.net/domenlightenment/YbtnZ*)

```
<!DOCTYPE html>
<html lang="en">
<body>

<p id="p1"></p>
<p id="p2"> </p>

<script>

console.log(document.querySelector('#p1').firstChild) //logs null
console.log(document.querySelector('#p2').firstChild.nodeName) //logs #text

</script>
</body>
</html>
```

Don't forget that whitespace and text characters in the DOM are typically represented by a text node. This of course means that carriage returns are considered text nodes. In the following code, I log a carriage return highlighting the fact that this type of character is a text node.

Live code (*http://jsfiddle.net/domenlightenment/9FEzq*)

```
<!DOCTYPE html>
<html lang="en">
<body>

<p id="p1"></p> /* yes there is a carriage return text node before this comment,
                even this comment is a node */
<p id="p2"></p>
```

```
<script>

console.log(document.querySelector('#p1').nextSibling) //logs Text

</script>
</body>
</html>
```

The reality is that if you can input the character or whitespace into an HTML document using a keyboard, it can potentially be interpreted as a text node. If you think about it, unless you minimize/compress the HTML document, the average HTML page contains a great deal of whitespace and carriage return text nodes.

7.4 Creating and Injecting Text Nodes

Text nodes are created automatically for us when a browser interprets an HTML document, and a corresponding DOM is built based on the contents of the document. After this automation, it's also possible to programmatically create Text nodes using create TextNode(). In the following code, I create a text node and then inject that node into the live DOM tree.

Live code (*http://jsfiddle.net/domenlightenment/xC9q3*)

```
<!DOCTYPE html>
<html lang="en">
<body>

<div></div>

<script>

var textNode = document.createTextNode('Hi');
document.querySelector('div').appendChild(textNode);

console.log(document.querySelector('div').innerText); // logs Hi

</script>
</body>
</html>
```

Keep in mind that we can also inject text nodes into programmatically created DOM structures. In the following code, I place a text node inside a <p> element before I inject it into the live DOM.

```
<!DOCTYPE html>
<html lang="en">

<div></div>

<body>

<script>

var elementNode = document.createElement('p');
var textNode = document.createTextNode('Hi');
elementNode.appendChild(textNode);
document.querySelector('div').appendChild(elementNode);

console.log(document.querySelector('div').innerHTML); //logs <div>Hi</div>

</script>
</body>
</html>
```

7.5 Getting a Text Node Value with .data or nodeValue

The text value/data represented by a Text node can be extracted from the node by using the .data or nodeValue property. Both of these return the text contained in a Text node. In the following code, I demonstrate both of these to retrieve the value contained in the <div>.

Live code (*http://jsfiddle.net/domenlightenment/dPLkx*)

```
<!DOCTYPE html>
<html lang="en">

<p>Hi, <strong>cody</strong></p><body>

<script>

console.log(document.querySelector('p').firstChild.data); //logs 'Hi,'
console.log(document.querySelector('p').firstChild.nodeValue); //logs 'Hi,'

</script>
</body>
</html>
```

Notice that the <p> contains two Text nodes and two Element (i.e., <strong>) nodes. Also note that we are only getting the value of the first child node contained in the <p>.

Note

Getting the length of the characters contained in a text node is as simple as accessing the length property of the node itself or the actual text value/data of the node (i.e., document.querySelector('p').first Child.length or document.querySelector('p').firstChild.da ta.length or document.querySelector('p').firstChild.nodeVal ue.length).

7.6 Manipulating Text Nodes with appendData(), deleteData(), insertData(), replaceData(), and subStringData()

The CharacterData object from which Text nodes inherit methods provides the following methods for manipulating and extracting subvalues from Text node values:

- appendData()
- deleteData()
- insertData()
- replaceData()
- subStringData()

Each of these is leveraged in the following code example.

Live code (*http://jsfiddle.net/domenlightenment/B6AC6*)

```
<!DOCTYPE html>
<html lang="en">

<p>Go big Blue Blue<body>

<script>

var pElementText = document.querySelector('p').firstChild;

//add !
pElementText.appendData('!');
console.log(pElementText.data);

//remove first 'Blue'
pElementText.deleteData(7,5);
console.log(pElementText.data);

//insert it back 'Blue'
pElementText.insertData(7,'Blue ');
console.log(pElementText.data);
```

```
//replace first 'Blue' with 'Bunny'
pElementText.replaceData(7,5,'Bunny ');
console.log(pElementText.data);

//extract substring 'Blue Bunny'
console.log(pElementText.substringData(7,10));

</script>
</body>
</html>
```

Note
These same manipulation and subextraction methods can be leveraged
by Comment nodes.

7.7 When Multiple Sibling Text Nodes Occur

Typically, immediate sibling Text nodes do not occur, because DOM trees created by
browsers intelligently combine text nodes. However, two cases exist that make sibling
text nodes possible. The first case is rather obvious. If a text node contains an Element
node (e.g., <p>Hi, cody welcome!</p>), the text will be split into
the proper node groupings. It's best to look at a code example, as this might sound more
complicated than it really is. In the following code, the content of the <p> element is not
a single Text node; it is in fact three nodes: a Text node, an Element node, and another
Text node.

Live code (*http://jsfiddle.net/domenlightenment/2ZCn3*)

```
<!DOCTYPE html>
<html lang="en">
<body>

<p>Hi, <strong>cody</strong> welcome!</p>

<script>

var pElement = document.querySelector('p');

console.log(pElement.childNodes.length); //logs 3

console.log(pElement.firstChild.data); // is text node or 'Hi, '
console.log(pElement.firstChild.nextSibling); // is Element node or <strong>
console.log(pElement.lastChild.data); // is text node or ' welcome!'

</script>
</body>
</html>
```

The next case occurs when we are programmatically adding Text nodes to an element we created in our code. In the following code, I create a <p> element and then append two Text nodes to this element. This results in sibling Text nodes.

Live code (*http://jsfiddle.net/domenlightenment/jk3Jn*)

```
<!DOCTYPE html>
<html lang="en">
<body>

<script>

var pElementNode = document.createElement('p');
var textNodeHi = document.createTextNode('Hi ');
var textNodeCody = document.createTextNode('Cody');

pElementNode.appendChild(textNodeHi);
pElementNode.appendChild(textNodeCody);

document.querySelector('div').appendChild(pElementNode);

console.log(document.querySelector('div p').childNodes.length); //logs 2

</script>
</body>
</html>
```

7.8 Using textContent to Remove Markup and Return All Child Text Nodes

The textContent property can be used to get all child text nodes, as well as to set the contents of a node to a specific Text node. When it's used on a node to get the textual content of the node, it will return a concatenated string of all text nodes contained with the node on which you call the method. This functionality makes it very easy to extract all text nodes from an HTML document. In the following code, I extract all the text contained within the <body> element. Notice that textContent gathers not just immediate child text nodes, but all child text nodes no matter the depth of encapsulation inside the node on which the method is called:

```
<!DOCTYPE html>
<html lang="en">
<body>
<h1> Dude</h2>
<p>you <strong>rock!</strong></p>
<script>

console.log(document.body.textContent); /* logs 'Dude you rock!' with some added
                                           white space */
```

```
</script>
</body>
</html>
```

When `textContent` is used to set the text contained within a node, it will remove all child nodes first, replacing them with a single `Text` node. In the following code, I replace all the nodes inside the `<div>` element with a single `Text` node.

Live code (*http://jsfiddle.net/domenlightenment/m766T*)

```
<!DOCTYPE html>
<html lang="en">
<body>
<div>
<h1> Dude</h2>
<p>you <strong>rock!</strong></p>
</div>
<script>

document.body.textContent = 'You don\'t rock!'
console.log(document.querySelector('div').textContent); //logs 'You don't rock!'

</script>
</body>
</html>
```

Notes

`textContent` returns `null` if used on a document or doctype node.

`textContent` returns the contents from `<script>` and `<style>` elements.

7.9 The Difference Between textContent and innerText

Most modern browsers, except Firefox, support a seemingly similar property to `text Content`, named `innerText`. However, these properties are not the same. You should be aware of the following differences between `textContent` and `innerText`:

- `innerText` is aware of CSS. So, if you have hidden text, `innerText` ignores this text, whereas `textContent` does not.

- Because `innerText` cares about CSS, it will trigger a reflow, whereas `textContent` will not.

- `innerText` ignores the `Text` nodes contained in `<script>` and `<style>` elements.

- `innerText`, unlike `textContent`, will normalize the text that is returned. Just think of `textContent` as returning exactly what is in the document, with the markup removed. This will include whitespace, line breaks, and carriage returns.

- innerText is considered to be nonstandard and browser-specific while textContent is implemented from the DOM specifications.

If you intend to use innerText, you'll have to create a workaround for Firefox.

7.10 Using normalize() to Combine Sibling Text Nodes into One Text Node

Sibling Text nodes are typically only encountered when text is programmatically added to the DOM. To eliminate sibling Text nodes that contain no Element nodes, we can use normalize(). This will concatenate sibling text nodes in the DOM into a single Text node. In the following code, I create sibling text, append it to the DOM, and then normalize it.

Live code (*http://jsfiddle.net/domenlightenment/LG9WR*)

```
<!DOCTYPE html>
<html lang="en">
<body>
<div></div>
<script>

var pElementNode = document.createElement('p');
var textNodeHi = document.createTextNode('Hi');
var textNodeCody = document.createTextNode('Cody');

pElementNode.appendChild(textNodeHi);
pElementNode.appendChild(textNodeCody);

document.querySelector('div').appendChild(pElementNode);

console.log(document.querySelector('p').childNodes.length); //logs 2

document.querySelector('div').normalize(); //combine our sibling text nodes

console.log(document.querySelector('p').childNodes.length); //logs 1

</script>
</body>
</html>
```

7.11 Using splitText() to Split a Text Node

When splitText() is called on a Text node, it will alter the text node on which it's being called (leaving the text up to the offset) and return a new Text node that contains the text split off from the original text based on the offset. In the following code, the text node Hey Yo! is split after Hey, and Hey is left in the DOM while Yo! is turned into a new text node and returned by the splitText() method.

Live code (*http://jsfiddle.net/domenlightenment/Tz5ce*)

```
<!DOCTYPE html>
<html lang="en">
<body>

<p>Hey Yo!</p>

<script>

//returns a new text node, taken from the DOM
console.log(document.querySelector('p').firstChild.splitText(4).data); //logs Yo!

//What remains in the DOM...
console.log(document.querySelector('p').firstChild.textContent); //logs Hey

</script>
</body>
</html>
```

CHAPTER 8
DocumentFragment Nodes

8.1 DocumentFragment Object Overview

The creation and use of a `DocumentFragment` node provides a lightweight document DOM that is external to the live DOM tree. Think of a `DocumentFragment` as an empty document template that acts just like the live DOM tree, but only lives in memory, and its child nodes can easily be manipulated in memory and then appended to the live DOM.

8.2 Using createDocumentFragment() to Create DocumentFragments

In the following code, a `DocumentFragment` is created by using `createDocumentFragment()`, and `<li>`s are appended to the fragment.

Live code (*http://jsfiddle.net/domenlightenment/6e3uX*)

```
<!DOCTYPE html>
<html lang="en">
<body>

<script>

var docFrag = document.createDocumentFragment();

["blue", "green", "red", "blue", "pink"].forEach(function(e) {
    var li = document.createElement("li");
    li.textContent = e;
    docFrag.appendChild(li);
});

console.log(docFrag.textContent); //logs bluegreenredbluepink
```

```
    </script>
  </body>
</html>
```

Using a document fragment to create node structures in memory is extremely efficient when it comes time to inject the document fragment into live node structures.

You might wonder what is the advantage to using a document fragment over simply creating (via createElement()) a <div> in memory and working within this <div> to create a DOM structure. Here are the differences between the two:

- A document fragment may contain any kind of node (except <body> or <html>), whereas an element may not.
- The document fragment itself is not added to the DOM when you append a fragment. The contents of the node are. This is in contrast to appending an element node in which the element itself is part of the append operation.
- When a document fragment is appended to the DOM, it transfers from the document fragment to the place where it is appended. It's no longer in memory in the place you created it. This is not true for element nodes that are used to contain nodes only briefly and then are moved to the live DOM.

8.3 Adding a DocumentFragment to the Live DOM

When you pass a document fragment argument to the appendChild() and insert Before() node methods, the child nodes of the document fragment are transported as child nodes to the DOM node on which the methods are called. In the following code, I create a document fragment, add some <li>s to it, and then append these new element nodes to the live DOM tree by using appendChild().

Live code (*http://jsfiddle.net/domenlightenment/Z2LpU*)

```
<!DOCTYPE html>
<html lang="en">
<body>

<ul></ul>

<script>

var ulElm = document.queryselector('ul');
var docFrag = document.createDocumentFragment();

["blue", "green", "red", "blue", "pink"].forEach(function(e) {
    var li = document.createElement("li");
    li.textContent = e;
    docFrag.appendChild(li);
});
```

```
ulElm.appendChild(docFrag);

//logs <ul><li>blue</li><li>green</li><li>red</li><li>blue</li><li>pink</li></ul>
console.log(document.body.innerHTML);

</script>
</body>
</html>
```

Note

Document fragments passed as arguments to inserting node methods will insert the entire child node structure, ignoring the document fragment node itself.

8.4 Using innerHTML on a Document Fragment

Creating a DOM structure in memory using node methods can be verbose and labor-intensive. One way around this is to create a document fragment, append a `<div>` to this fragment because innerHTML does not work on document fragments, and then use the innerHTML property to update the fragment with a string of HTML. As a result of this, a DOM structure is crafted from the HTML string. In the following code, I construct a DOM structure that I can then treat as a tree of nodes and not just a JavaScript string.

Live code (*http://jsfiddle.net/domenlightenment/4W9sH*)

```
<!DOCTYPE html>
<html lang="en">
<body>

<script>

//create a <div> and document fragment
var divElm = document.createElement('div');
var docFrag = document.createDocumentFragment();

//append div to document fragment
docFrag.appendChild(divElm);

//create a DOM structure from a string
docFrag.querySelector('div').innerHTML = '<ul><li>foo</li><li>bar</li></ul>';

/* the string becomes a DOM structure I can call methods on like
querySelectorAll() */
//Just don't forget the DOM structure is wrapped in a <div>
console.log(docFrag.querySelectorAll('li').length); //logs 2
```

```
</script>
</body>
</html>
```

When it comes time to append a DOM structure created using a document fragment and <div>, you'll want to append the structure, skipping the injection of the <div>.

Live code (*http://jsfiddle.net/domenlightenment/kkyKJ*)

```
<!DOCTYPE html>
<html lang="en">
<body>

<div></div>

<script>

//create a <div> and document fragment
var divElm = document.createElement('div');
var docFrag = document.createDocumentFragment();

//append div to document fragment
docFrag.appendChild(divElm);

//create a DOM structure from a string
docFrag.querySelector('div').innerHTML = '<ul><li>foo</li><li>bar</li></ul>';

//append, starting with the first child node contained inside of the <div>
document.querySelector('div').appendChild(
  docFrag.querySelector('div').firstChild);

//logs <ul><li>foo</li><li>bar</li></ul>
console.log(document.querySelector('div').innerHTML);

</script>
</body>
</html>
```

Note

In addition to DocumentFragment, we have DOMParser (*http://bit.ly/11dfxzT*) to look forward to. DOMParser can parse HTML stored in a string into a DOM document (*https://developer.mozilla.org/en/DOM/document*). It's only supported in Opera and Firefox at the time of this writing, but a polyfill is available (*https://gist.github.com/1129031*). Of course, if you need a standalone HTML-to-DOM script, try domify (*https://github.com/component/domify*).

8.5 Leaving Fragments Containing Nodes in Memory by Cloning

When appending a document fragment, the nodes contained in the fragment are moved from the fragment to the structure you are appending to. To leave the contents of a fragment in memory so that the nodes remain after appending, simply use clone Node() and clone the document fragment when appending. In the following code, instead of transporting the <li>s from the document fragment, I clone the <li>s, which keeps the <li>s being cloned in memory inside the document fragment node.

Live code (*http://jsfiddle.net/domenlightenment/bcJGS*)

```html
<!DOCTYPE html>
<html lang="en">
<body>

<ul></ul>

<script>
//create ul element and document fragment
var ulElm = document.querySelector('ul');
var docFrag = document.createDocumentFragment();

//append li's to document fragment
["blue", "green", "red", "blue", "pink"].forEach(function(e) {
    var li = document.createElement("li");
    li.textContent = e;
    docFrag.appendChild(li);
});

//append cloned document fragment to ul in live DOM
ulElm.appendChild(docFrag.cloneNode(true));

//logs <li>blue</li><li>green</li><li>red</li><li>blue</li><li>pink</li>
console.log(document.querySelector('ul').innerHTML);

//logs [li,li,li,li,li]
console.log(docFrag.childNodes);

</script>
</body>
</html>
```

CSS Stylesheets and CSS Rules

9.1 CSS Stylesheet Overview

A stylesheet is added to an HTML document by using either the `HTMLLinkElement` node (i.e., `<link href="stylesheet.css" rel="stylesheet" type="text/css">`) to include an external stylesheet or the `HTMLStyleElement` node (i.e., `<style></style>`) to define a stylesheet inline. In the following HTML document, both of these `Element` nodes are in the DOM and I verify which constructor constructs these nodes.

Live code (*http://jsfiddle.net/domenlightenment/yPYyC*)

```
<!DOCTYPE html>
<html lang="en">
<head>

<link id="linkElement"
  href="http://yui.yahooapis.com/3.3.0/build/cssreset/reset-min.css"
  rel="stylesheet" type="text/css">

<style id="styleElement">
body{background-color:#fff;}
</style>

</head>
<body>

<script>

//logs function HTMLLinkElement() { [native code] }
console.log(document.querySelector('#linkElement').constructor);

//logs function HTMLStyleElement() { [native code] }
console.log(document.querySelector('#styleElement').constructor);
```

```
</script>
</body>
</html>
```

Once a stylesheet is added to an HTML document, it's represented by the CSSStyle sheet object. Each CSS rule (e.g., body{background-color:red;}) inside a stylesheet is represented by a CSSStyleRule object. In the following code, I verify which constructor constructed the stylesheet and each CSS rule (selector and its CSS properties and values) in the stylesheet.

Live code (*http://jsfiddle.net/domenlightenment/UpLzm*)

```
<!DOCTYPE html>
<html lang="en">
<head>

<style id="styleElement">
body{background-color:#fff;}
</style>

</head>
<body>

<script>

/* logs function CSSStyleSheet() { [native code] } because this object is the
stylesheet itself */
console.log(document.querySelector('#styleElement').sheet.constructor);

/* logs function CSSStyleRule() { [native code] } because this object is the rule
inside of the stylesheet */
console.log(document.querySelector(
  '#styleElement').sheet.cssRules[0].constructor);

</script>
</body>
</html>
```

Keep in mind that selecting the element that includes the stylesheet (i.e., <link> or <style>) is not the same as accessing the actual object (CSSStylesheet) that represents the stylesheet itself.

9.2 Accessing All Stylesheets (i.e., CSSStylesheet Objects) in the DOM

document.styleSheets gives access to a list of all stylesheet objects (a.k.a. CSSStyle sheet objects) explicitly linked (i.e., <link>) or embedded (i.e., <style>) in an HTML document. In the following code, styleSheets is leveraged to gain access to all the stylesheets contained in the document:

```
<!DOCTYPE html>
<html lang="en">
<head>

<link href="http://yui.yahooapis.com/3.3.0/build/cssreset/reset-min.css"
  rel="stylesheet" type="text/css">

<style>
body{background-color:red;}
</style>

</head>
<body>

<script>

console.log(document.styleSheets.length); //logs 2
console.log(document.styleSheets[0]); // the <link>
console.log(document.styleSheets[1]); // the <style>

</script>
</body>
</html>
```

Notes

styleSheets is live just like most other nodelists.

The length property returns the number of stylesheets contained in the list, starting at the 0 index (i.e., document.styleSheets.length).

The stylesheets included in a styleSheets list typically include any stylesheets created using the <style> element or using a <link> element where rel is set to stylesheet.

In addition to using styleSheets to access a document's stylesheets, it's possible to access a stylesheet in an HTML document by first selecting the element in the DOM (<style> or <link>) and then using the .sheet property to gain access to the CSS Stylesheet object. In the following code, I access the stylesheets in the HTML document by first selecting the element used to include the stylesheet and then leveraging the .sheet property.

Live code (*http://jsfiddle.net/domenlightenment/jFwKw*)

```
<!DOCTYPE html>
<html lang="en">
<head>
```

```
<link id="linkElement"
  href="http://yui.yahooapis.com/3.3.0/build/cssreset/reset-min.css"
  rel="stylesheet" type="text/css">

<style id="styleElement">
body{background-color:#fff;}
</style>

</head>
<body>

<script>

//get CSSStylesheet object for <link>
console.log(document.querySelector('#linkElement').sheet);
  //same as document.styleSheets[0]

//get CSSStylesheet object for <style>
console.log(document.querySelector('#styleElement').sheet);
  //same as document.styleSheets[1]

</script>
</body>
</html>
```

9.3 CSSStyleSheet Properties and Methods

To get accurate information pertaining to the available properties and methods on a
CSSStyleSheet node, it's best to ignore the specification and to ask the browser what is
available. Examine the arrays created in the following code detailing the properties and
methods available from a CSSStyleSheet node.

Live code (*http://jsfiddle.net/domenlightenment/kNyL2*)

```
<!DOCTYPE html>
<html lang="en">
<head>

<style id="styleElement">
body{background-color:#fff;}
</style>

</head>
<body>

<script>

var styleSheet = document.querySelector('#styleElement').sheet;

//text own properties
console.log(Object.keys(styleSheet).sort());
```

```
//text own properties and inherited properties
var styleSheetPropertiesIncludeInherited = [];
for(var p in styleSheet){
    styleSheetPropertiesIncludeInherited.push(p);
}
console.log(styleSheetPropertiesIncludeInherited.sort());

//text inherited properties only
var styleSheetPropertiesOnlyInherited = [];
for(var p in styleSheet){
    if(!styleSheet.hasOwnProperty(p)){
        styleSheetPropertiesOnlyInherited.push(p);
    }
}
console.log(styleSheetPropertiesOnlyInherited.sort());

</script>
</body>
</html>
```

A CSSStylesheet object accessed from a styleSheets list or via the .sheet property has the following properties and methods:

- disabled
- href
- media
- ownerNode
- parentStylesheet
- title
- type
- cssRules
- ownerRule
- deleteRule
- insertRule

Note

href, media, ownerNode, parentStylesheet, title, and type are read-only properties. You can't provide new values for them.

9.4 CSSStyleRule Overview

A `CSSStyleRule` object represents each CSS rule contained in a stylesheet. Basically, a `CSSStyleRule` is the interface to the CSS properties and values attached to a selector. In the following code, I programmatically access the details of each rule contained in the inline stylesheet by accessing the `CSSStyleRule` object that represents the CSS rule in the stylesheet.

Live code (*http://jsfiddle.net/domenlightenment/fPVS8*)

```
<!DOCTYPE html>
<html lang="en">
<head>

<style id="styleElement">
body{background-color:#fff;margin:20px;} /* this is a css rule */
p{line-height:1.4em; color:blue;} /* this is a css rule */
</style>

</head>
<body>

<script>

var sSheet = document.querySelector('#styleElement').sheet;

console.log(sSheet.cssRules[0].cssText); /* logs "body { background-color: red;
                                           margin: 20px; }" */
console.log(sSheet.cssRules[1].cssText); /* logs "p { line-height: 1.4em;
                                           color: blue; }" */

</script>
</body>
</html>
```

9.5 CSSStyleRule Properties and Methods

To get accurate information pertaining to the available properties and methods on a `CSSStyleRule` node, it's best to ignore the specification and to ask the browser what is available. Examine the arrays created in the following code detailing the properties and methods available from a `CSSStyleRule` node.

Live code (*http://jsfiddle.net/domenlightenment/hCX3U*)

```
<!DOCTYPE html>
<html lang="en">
<head>
```

```
<style id="styleElement">
body{background-color:#fff;}
</style>

</head>
<body>

<script>

var styleSheetRule = document.querySelector('#styleElement').sheet.cssRule;

//text own properties
console.log(Object.keys(styleSheetRule).sort());

//text own properties and inherited properties
var styleSheetPropertiesIncludeInherited = [];
for(var p in styleSheetRule){
    styleSheetRulePropertiesIncludeInherited.push(p);
}
console.log(styleSheetRulePropertiesIncludeInherited.sort());

//text inherited properties only
var styleSheetRulePropertiesOnlyInherited = [];
for(var p in styleSheetRule){
    if(!styleSheetRule.hasOwnProperty(p)){
        styleSheetRulePropertiesOnlyInherited.push(p);
    }
}
console.log(styleSheetRulePropertiesOnlyInherited.sort());

</script>
</body>
</html>
```

Scripting the rules (e.g., body{background-color:red;}) contained inside a stylesheet is made possible by the cssRules object. This object provides the following properties:

- cssText
- parentRule
- parentStylesheet
- selectorText
- style
- type

9.6 Using cssRules to Get a List of CSS Rules in a Stylesheet

As previously discussed, the styleSheets list provides a list of stylesheets contained in a document. The cssRules list provides a list (a.k.a. cssRulesList) of all the CSS rules (i.e., CSSStyleRule objects) in a specific stylesheet. The following code logs a cssRules list to the console.

Live code (*http://jsfiddle.net/domenlightenment/qKqhJ*)

```
<!DOCTYPE html>
<html lang="en">
<head>

<style id="styleElement">
body{background-color:#fff;margin:20px;}
p{line-height:1.4em; color:blue;}
</style>

</head>
<body>

<script>

var sSheet = document.querySelector('#styleElement').sheet;

/* arraylike list containing all of the CSSrule objects representing each CSS
rule in the stylesheet */
console.log(sSheet.cssRules);

console.log(sSheet.cssRules.length); //logs 2

//rules are indexed in a CSSRules list starting at a 0 index
console.log(sSheet.cssRules[0]); //logs first rule
console.log(sSheet.cssRules[1]); //logs second rule

</script>
</body>
</html>
```

9.7 Using insertRule() and deleteRule() to Insert and Delete CSS Rules in a Stylesheet

The insertRule() and deleteRule() methods provide the ability to programmatically manipulate the CSS rules in a stylesheet. In the following code, I use insertRule() to add the CSS rule p{color:red} to the inline stylesheet at index 1. Remember, the CSS rules in a stylesheet are numerically indexed starting at 0. So when you insert a new rule at index 1, the current rule at index 1 (i.e., p{font-size:50px;}) is pushed to index 2.

```
<!DOCTYPE html>
<html lang="en">
<head>

<style id="styleElement">
p{line-height:1.4em; color:blue;} /* index 0 */
p{font-size:50px;} /* index 1 */
</style>

</head>
<body>

<p>Hi</p>

<script>

//add a new CSS rule at index 1 in the inline stylesheet
document.querySelector('#styleElement').sheet.insertRule('p{color:red}',1);

//verify it was added
console.log(document.querySelector('#styleElement').sheet.cssRules[1].cssText);

//Delete what we just added
document.querySelector('#styleElement').sheet.deleteRule(1);

//verify it was removed
console.log(document.querySelector('#styleElement').sheet.cssRules[1].cssText);

</script>
</body>
</html>
```

Deleting or removing a rule is as simple as calling the `deleteRule()` method on a stylesheet and passing it the index of the rule in the stylesheet to be deleted.

Note

Inserting and deleting rules is not a common practice given the difficulty around managing the cascade and using a numeric indexing system to update a stylesheet (i.e., determining at what index a style is located without previewing the contents of the stylesheet itself). It's much simpler working with CSS rules in CSS and HTML files before they are served to a client than programmatically altering them in the client after the fact.

9.8 Using the .style Property to Edit the Value of a CSSStyleRule

Just as we have the .style property that facilitates the manipulation of inline styles on element nodes, we also have a .style property for CSSStyleRule objects that orchestrates the same manipulation of styles in stylesheets. In the following code, I leverage the .style property to set and get the value of CSS rules contained in the inline stylesheet.

Live code (*http://jsfiddle.net/domenlightenment/aZ9CQ*)

```
<!DOCTYPE html>
<html lang="en">
<head>

<style id="styleElement">
p{color:blue;}
strong{color:green;}
</style>

</head>
<body>

<p>Hey <strong>Dude!</strong></p>

<script>

var styleSheet = document.querySelector('#styleElement').sheet;

//Set css rules in stylesheet
styleSheet.cssRules[0].style.color = 'red';
styleSheet.cssRules[1].style.color = 'purple';

//Get css rules
console.log(styleSheet.cssRules[0].style.color); //logs 'red'
console.log(styleSheet.cssRules[1].style.color); //logs 'purple'

</script>
</body>
</html>
```

9.9 Creating a New Inline CSS Stylesheet

To craft a new stylesheet on the fly after an HTML page is loaded, one only has to create a new <style> node, use innerHTML to add CSS rules to this node, and then append the <style> node to the HTML document. In the following code, I programmatically craft a stylesheet and add the body{color:red} CSS rule to it, then append the stylesheet to the DOM.

Live code (*http://jsfiddle.net/domenlightenment/bKXAk*)

```
<!DOCTYPE html>
<html lang="en">
<head></head>
<body>

<p>Hey <strong>Dude!</strong></p>

<script>

var styleElm = document.createElement('style');
styleElm.innerHTML = 'body{color:red}';

//notice markup in the document changed to red from our new inline stylesheet
document.querySelector('head').appendChild(styleElm);

</script>
</body>
</html>
```

9.10 Programmatically Adding External Stylesheets to an HTML Document

To add a CSS file to an HTML document programmatically, you create a `<link>` element node with the appropriate attributes and then append the `<link>` element node to the DOM. In the following code, I programmatically include an external stylesheet by crafting a new `<link>` element and appending it to the DOM.

Live code (*http://jsfiddle.net/domenlightenment/dtwgC*)

```
<!DOCTYPE html>
<html lang="en">
<head></head>
<body>

<script>

//create and add attributes to <link>
var linkElm = document.createElement('link');
linkElm.setAttribute('rel', 'stylesheet');
linkElm.setAttribute('type', 'text/css');
linkElm.setAttribute('id', 'linkElement');
linkElm.setAttribute('href',
  'http://yui.yahooapis.com/3.3.0/build/cssreset/reset-min.css');

//Append to the DOM
document.head.appendChild(linkElm);
```

```
//confirm its addition to the DOM
console.log(document.querySelector('#linkElement'));

</script>
</body>
</html>
```

9.11 Using the .disabled Property to Disable/Enable Stylesheets

Using the .disabled property of a CSSStylesheet object, it's possible to enable or disable a stylesheet. In the following code, I access the current disabled value of each stylesheet in the document and then proceed to disable each stylesheet, leveraging the .disabled property.

Live code (*http://jsfiddle.net/domenlightenment/L952Z*)

```
<!DOCTYPE html>
<html lang="en">
<head>

<link id="linkElement"
  href="http://yui.yahooapis.com/3.3.0/build/cssreset/reset-min.css"
  rel="stylesheet" type="text/css">

<style id="styleElement">
body{color:red;}
</style>

</head>
<body>

<script>

//Get current boolean disabled value
console.log(document.querySelector('#linkElement').disabled); //log 'false'
console.log(document.querySelector('#styleElement').disabled); //log 'false'

//Set disabled value, which of course disables all styles for this document
document.document.querySelector('#linkElement').disabled = true;
document.document.querySelector('#styleElement').disabled = true;

</script>
</body>
</html>
```

Note

Disabled is not an available attribute of a `<link>` or `<style>` element, according to the specification. Trying to add this as an attribute in the HTML document itself will fail (and likely will cause parsing errors where styles are ignored) in the majority of modern browsers in use today.

JavaScript in the DOM

10.1 Inserting and Executing JavaScript Overview

JavaScript can be inserted into an HTML document by including external JavaScript files or writing page-level inline JavaScript, which is basically the contents of an external JavaScript file literally embedded in the HTML page as a text node. Don't confuse element inline JavaScript contained in attribute event handlers (i.e., `<div on click="alert('yo')"></div>`) with page inline JavaScript (i.e., `<script>alert('hi') </script>`).

Both methods of inserting JavaScript into an HTML document require the use of a `<script>` (*http://bit.ly/VsS59S*) element node (*http://bit.ly/VsS59S*). The `<script>` element can contain JavaScript code or can be used to link to external JavaScript files via the src attribute. Both methods are explored in the following code example.

Live code (*http://jsfiddle.net/domenlightenment/g6T5F*)

```
<!DOCTYPE html>
<html lang="en">
<body>

<!-- external, cross domain JavaScript include -->
<script src=
  "http://cdnjs.cloudflare.com/ajax/libs/underscore.js/1.3.3/underscore-min.js">
</script>

<!-- page inline JavaScript -->
<script>
console.log('hi');
</script>

</body>
</html>
```

Notes

It's possible to insert and execute JavaScript in the DOM by placing the JavaScript in an element attribute event handler (i.e., `<div on click="alert('yo')"></div>`) and using the `javascript:` protocol (e.g., `<a href="javascript:alert('yo')"></a>`), but this is no longer considered a modern practice.

Trying to include an external JavaScript file and writing page inline JavaScript using the same `<script>` element will result in the page inline JavaScript being ignored and the external JavaScript file being downloaded and executed.

Self-closing script tags (i.e., `<script src="" />`) should be avoided, unless you are rocking some old-school XHTML.

The `<script>` element does not have any required attributes but offers the following optional attributes: `async`, `charset`, `defer`, `src`, and `type`.

Page inline JavaScript produces a text node, which permits the usage of `innerHTML` and `textContent` to retrieve the contents of a line `<script>`. However, appending a new text node made up of JavaScript code to the DOM after the browser has already parsed the DOM will not execute the new JavaScript code. It simply replaces the text.

If JavaScript code contains the string `'</script>'` you will have to escape the closing `'/'` with `'<\/script>'` so that the parser does not think this is the real closing `</script>` element.

10.2 JavaScript Is Parsed Synchronously by Default

By default, when the DOM is being parsed and it encounters a `<script>` element, it will stop parsing the document, block any further rendering and downloading, and execute the JavaScript. Because this behavior is blocking and does not permit parallel parsing of the DOM or execution of JavaScript, it's considered to be synchronous. If the JavaScript is external to the HTML document, the blocking is exacerbated, because the JavaScript must first be downloaded before it can be parsed. In the following code example, I comment on what is occurring during browser rendering when the browser encounters several `<script>` elements in the DOM.

Live code (*http://jsfiddle.net/domenlightenment/rF3Lh*)

```
<!DOCTYPE html>
<html lang="en">
<body>

<!-- stop document parsing, block document parsing, load js, execute js, then
resume document parsing... -->
<script src=
  "http://cdnjs.cloudflare.com/ajax/libs/underscore.js/1.3.3/underscore-min.js">
```

```
</script>

<!-- stop document parsing, block document parsing, execute js, then resume
document parsing... -->
<script>console.log('hi');</script>


</body>
</html>
```

You should make note of the differences between inline scripts and external scripts as they pertain to the loading phase.

Note

The default blocking nature of a `<script>` element can have a significant effect on the performance and perceived performance of the visual rendering of an HTML web page. If you have a couple of script elements at the start of an HTML page, nothing else is happening (e.g., DOM parsing and resource loading) until each one is downloaded and executed sequentially.

10.3 Using defer to Defer the Downloading and Execution of External JavaScript

The `<script>` element has an attribute called `defer` that will defer the blocking, downloading, and execution of an external JavaScript file until the browser has parsed the closing `</html>` node. When you use this attribute, you simply defer what normally occurs when a web browser encounters a `<script>` node. In the following code, I defer each external JavaScript file until the final `<html>` is encountered.

Live code (*http://jsfiddle.net/domenlightenment/HDegp*)

```
<!DOCTYPE html>
<html lang="en">
<body>

<!-- defer, don't block just ignore this until the <html> element node is
parsed -->
<script defer src=
  "http://cdnjs.cloudflare.com/ajax/libs/underscore.js/1.3.3/underscore-min.js">
</script>

<!-- defer, don't block just ignore this until the <html> element node is
parsed -->
<script defer src=
  "http://cdnjs.cloudflare.com/ajax/libs/jquery/1.7.2/jquery.min.js">
</script>
```

```
<!-- defer, don't block just ignore this until the <html> element node is
parsed -->
<script defer src=
  "http://cdnjs.cloudflare.com/ajax/libs/jquery-mousewheel/3.0.6/
  jquery.mousewheel.min.js">
</script>

<script>
/* We know that jQuery is not available because this occurs before the closing
<html> element */
console.log(window['jQuery'] === undefined); //logs true

/* Only after everything is loaded can we safely conclude that jQuery was
loaded and parsed */
document.body.onload = function(){console.log(jQuery().jquery)}; //logs function
</script>

</body>
</html>
```

Notes

According to the specification, deferred scripts are supposed to be executed in document order and before the DOMContentLoaded event. However, adherence to this specification among modern browsers is inconsistent.

defer is a Boolean attribute; it does not have a value.

Some browsers support deferred inline scripts, but this is not common among modern browsers.

By using defer, the assumption is that document.write() is not being used in the JavaScript that will be deferred.

10.4 Using async to Asynchronously Download and Execute External JavaScript Files

The <script> element has an attribute called async that will override the sequential blocking nature of <script> elements when the DOM is being constructed by a web browser. By using this attribute, we are telling the browser to not block the construction of the HTML page (i.e., DOM parsing, including downloading other assets such as images, stylesheets, etc.) and to forego the sequential loading as well.

When you use the async attribute, the files are loaded in parallel and parsed in order of download once they are fully downloaded. In the following code, I comment on what is happening when the HTML document is being parsed and rendered by the web browser.

```
<!DOCTYPE html>
<html lang="en">
<body>

<!-- Don't block, just start downloading and then parse the file when it's done
downloading -->
<script async src=
  "http://cdnjs.cloudflare.com/ajax/libs/underscore.js/1.3.3/underscore-min.js">
</script>

<!-- Don't block, just start downloading and then parse the file when it's done
downloading -->
<script async src=
  "http://cdnjs.cloudflare.com/ajax/libs/jquery/1.7.2/jquery.min.js">
</script>

<!-- Don't block, just start downloading and then parse the file when it's done
downloading -->
<script async src=
  "http://cdnjs.cloudflare.com/ajax/libs/jquery-mousewheel/3.0.6/
  jquery.mousewheel.min.js">
</script>


<script>
// we have no idea if jQuery has been loaded yet likely not yet...
console.log(window['jQuery'] === undefined);//logs true

/* Only after everything is loaded can we safely conclude that jQuery was
loaded and parsed */
document.body.onload = function(){console.log(jQuery().jquery)};
</script>

</body>
</html>
```

Notes

IE 10 has support for `async`, but IE 9 does not.

A major drawback to using the `async` attribute is that JavaScript files potentially get parsed out of the order in which they are included in the DOM. This raises a dependency management issue.

`async` is a Boolean attribute; it does not have a value.

By using `async`, the assumption is that `document.write()` is not being used in the JavaScript that will be deferred.

The `async` attribute will trump the `defer` if both are used on a `<script>` element.

10.5 Using Dynamic <script> Elements to Force Asynchronous Downloading and Parsing of External JavaScript

A known hack for forcing a web browser into asynchronous JavaScript downloading and parsing without using the async attribute is to programmatically create <script> elements that include external JavaScript files and insert them in the DOM. In the following code, I programmatically create the <script> element node and then append it to the <body> element, which forces the browser to treat the <script> element asynchronously.

Live code (*http://jsfiddle.net/domenlightenment/du94d*)

```
<!DOCTYPE html>
<html lang="en">
<body>

<!-- Don't block, just start downloading and then parse the file when it's done
downloading -->
<script>
var underscoreScript = document.createElement("script");
underscoreScript.src =
  "http://cdnjs.cloudflare.com/ajax/libs/underscore.js/1.3.3/underscore-min.js";
document.body.appendChild(underscoreScript);
</script>

<!-- Don't block, just start downloading and then parse the file when it's done
downloading -->
<script>
var jqueryScript = document.createElement("script");
jqueryScript.src =
  "http://cdnjs.cloudflare.com/ajax/libs/jquery/1.7.2/jquery.min.js";
document.body.appendChild(jqueryScript);
</script>

<!-- Don't block, just start downloading and then parse the file when it's done
downloading -->
<script>
var mouseWheelScript = document.createElement("script");
mouseWheelScript.src =
  "http://cdnjs.cloudflare.com/ajax/libs/jquery-mousewheel/3.0.6/
  jquery.mousewheel.min.js";
document.body.appendChild(mouseWheelScript);
</script>

<script>
/* Only after everything is loaded can we safely conclude that jQuery was loaded
and parsed */
document.body.onload = function(){console.log(jQuery().jquery)};
</script>
```

```
</body>
</html>
```

Note

A major drawback to using dynamic `<script>` elements is that Java-Script files potentially get parsed out of the order in which they are included in the DOM. This raises a dependency management issue.

10.6 Using the onload Callback for Asynchronous `<script>`s so That We Know When They're Loaded

The `<script>` element supports a load event (*http://pieisgood.org/test/script-link-events/*) handler (i.e., `onload`) that will execute once an external JavaScript file has been loaded and executed. In the following code, I leverage the `onload` event to create a callback programmatically, notifying me when the JavaScript file has been downloaded and executed.

Live code (*http://jsfiddle.net/domenlightenment/XzAFx*)

```
<!DOCTYPE html>
<html lang="en">
<body>

<!-- Don't block, just start downloading and then parse the file when it's done
downloading -->
<script>
var underscoreScript = document.createElement("script");
underscoreScript.src =
  "http://cdnjs.cloudflare.com/ajax/libs/underscore.js/1.3.3/underscore-min.js";
underscoreScript.onload =
  function(){console.log('underscsore is loaded and executed');};
document.body.appendChild(underscoreScript);
</script>

<!-- Don't block, just start downloading and then parse the file when it's done
downloading -->
<script async src=
  "http://cdnjs.cloudflare.com/ajax/libs/jquery/1.7.2/jquery.min.js"
  onload="console.log('jQuery is loaded and exectuted');">
</script>

</body>
</html>
```

Note

The onload event is only the tip of the iceberg in terms of where on load is supported (*http://pieisgood.org/test/script-link-events/*); you also have use of onerror, load, and error.

10.7 Be Mindful of <script>s Placement in HTML for DOM Manipulation

Given a <script> element's synchronous nature, placing one in the <head> element of an HTML document presents a timing problem if the JavaScript execution is dependent on any of the DOM that precedes the <script>. In a nutshell, if JavaScript is executed at the beginning of a document that manipulates the DOM that precedes it, you are going to get a JavaScript error, as shown in the following code example:

```
<!DOCTYPE html>
<html lang="en">
<head>
<!-- stop parsing, block parsing, execute js then resume... -->
<script>
/* we can't script the body element yet, it's null, not even been parsed by the
browser, it's not in the DOM yet */
console.log(document.body.innerHTML); /* logs Uncaught TypeError: Cannot read
                                          property 'innerHTML' of null */
</script>
</head>
<body>
<strong>Hi</strong>
</body>
</html>
```

For this reason, many developers, myself included, will attempt to place all <script> elements before the closing </body> element. By doing this, you can rest assured that the DOM in front of the <script>s has been parsed and is ready for scripting. As well, this strategy will remove a dependency on DOM-ready events that can litter a code base.

10.8 Getting a List of <script>s in the DOM

The document.scripts property available from the document object provides a list (i.e., an HTMLCollection) of all the scripts currently in the DOM. In the following code, I leverage this property to gain access to each <script> element's src attributes:

```
<!DOCTYPE html>
<html lang="en">
<body>
<script src=
  "http://cdnjs.cloudflare.com/ajax/libs/underscore.js/1.3.3/underscore-min.js">
</script>
```

```
<script src=
  "http://cdnjs.cloudflare.com/ajax/libs/jquery/1.7.2/jquery.min.js">
</script>
<script src=
  "http://cdnjs.cloudflare.com/ajax/libs/jquery-mousewheel/3.0.6/
  jquery.mousewheel.min.js">
</script>

<script>
Array.prototype.slice.call(document.scripts).forEach(function(elm){
    console.log(elm);
});//will log each script element in the document
</script>

</body>
</html>
```

DOM Events

11.1 DOM Events Overview

An event, in terms of the DOM, is either a predefined or a custom moment in time that occurs in relationship to an element in the DOM, the document object, or the window object. These moments are typically predetermined and programmatically accounted for by associating functionality (i.e., handlers/callbacks) to occur when these moments in time come to pass. These moments can be initiated by the state of the UI (e.g., input is focused or something has been dragged), the state of the environment that is running the JavaScript program (e.g., a page is loaded or an XHR request has finished), or the state of the program itself (e.g., monitor all mouse clicks for 30 seconds after the page has loaded).

Setting up events can be accomplished using inline attribute event handlers, property event handlers, or the addEventListener() method. In the following code, I'm demonstrating these three patterns for setting up an event. All three patterns add a click event that is invoked whenever the <div> in the HTML document is clicked by the mouse.

Live code (*http://jsfiddle.net/domenlightenment/4EPjN*)

```html
<!DOCTYPE html>
<html lang="en">

<!-- inline attribute event handler pattern -->
<body onclick="console.log('fire/trigger attribute event handler')">

<div>click me</div>

<script>
var elementDiv = document.querySelector('div');
```

```
// property event handler pattern
elementDiv.onclick = function()
  {console.log('fire/trigger property event handler')};

//addEventListener method pattern
elementDiv.addEventListener('click',function()
  {console.log('fire/trigger addEventListener')}, false);
</script>
</body>
</html>
```

Notice that one of the events is attached to the <body> element. If you find it odd that the attribute event handler on the <body> fires by clicking the <div> element, consider that when the <div> is clicked, you are also clicking on the <body> element. Click anywhere but on the <div>, and you still see the attribute handler fire on the <body> element alone.

While all three of these patterns for attaching an event to the DOM programmatically schedule the event, only the addEventListener() provides a robust and organized solution. The inline attribute event handler mixes together JavaScript and HTML, and best practices advise keeping these things separate.

The downside to using a property event handler is that only one value can be assigned to the event property at a time. This means you can't add more than one property event handler to a DOM node when assigning events as property values. The following code shows an example of this by assigning a value to the onclick property twice; the last value set is used when the event is invoked.

Live code (*http://jsfiddle.net/domenlightenment/U8bWR*)

```
<!DOCTYPE html>
<html lang="en">
<body>

<div>click me</div>

<script>
var elementDiv = document.querySelector('div');

// property event handler
elementDiv.onclick = function()
  {console.log('I\'m first, but I get overridden/replaced')};

//overrides/replaces the prior value
elementDiv.onclick = function(){console.log('I win')};

</script>
</body>
</html>
```

Additionally, using event handlers inline on property event handlers can suffer from scoping nuances as one attempts to leverage the scope chain from the function that is invoked by the event. The addEventListener() method smooths out these issues, and we will use it throughout this chapter.

Notes

Element nodes typically support inline event handlers (e.g., <div on click=""></div>), property event handlers (e.g., document.querySe lector('div').onclick = function(){}), and the use of the addEventListener() method.

The Document node supports property event handlers (e.g., docu ment.onclick = function()) and the use of the addEventListen er() method.

The window object supports inline event handlers via the <body> or <frameset> element (e.g., <body onload=""></body>), property event handlers (e.g., window.load = function(){}), and the use of the addEventListener() method.

A property event handler historically has been referred to as a "DOM Level 0 event." And the addEventListener() is often referred to as a "DOM Level 2 event." This is rather confusing, considering that there is no Level 0 event or Level 1 event specification. Additionally, inline event handlers are known to be called "HTML event handlers."

11.2 DOM Event Types

In Tables 11-1 through 11-10, I detail the most common predefined events that can be attached to Element nodes, the document object, and the window object. Of course, not all events are directly applicable to the node or object they can be attached to. That is, just because you can attach the event without error, and most likely invoke the event (i.e., bubbling events like onchange to window), this does not mean that adding something like window.onchange is logical, given that this event, by design, was not meant for the window object.

Table 11-1. User interface events

Event type	Event interface	Description	Event targets	Bubbles?	Cancelable?
load	Event, UIEvent	Fires when an asset (HTML page, image, CSS, frameset, <object>, or JavaScript file) is loaded	Element, Document, win dow, XMLHttpRequest, XMLHttpRequestUp load	No	No

Event type	Event interface	Description	Event targets	Bubbles?	Cancelable?
unload	UIEvent	Fires when a user agent removes the resource (document, element, `defaultView`) or any depending resources (images, CSS file, etc.)	`window`, `<body>`, `<frameset>`	No	No
abort	Event, UIEvent	Fires when a resource (object/image) is stopped from loading before it is completely loaded	`Element`, `XMLHttpRequest`, `XMLHttpRequestUpload`	Yes	No
error	Event, UIEvent	Fires when a resource failed to load, or has been loaded but cannot be interpreted according to its semantics, such as an invalid image, a script execution error, or non-well-formed XML	`Element`, `XMLHttpRequest`, `XMLHttpRequestUpload`	Yes	No
resize	UIEvent	Fires when a document view has been resized; this event type is dispatched after all effects for that occurrence of resizing of that particular event target have been executed by the user agent	`window`, `<body>`, `<frameset>`	Yes	No
scroll	UIEvent	Fires when a user scrolls a document or an element	`Element`, `Document`, `window`	Yes	No
context menu	MouseEvent	Fires by right-clicking an element	`Element`	Yes	Yes

Table 11-2. Focus events

Event type	Event interface	Description	Events targets	Bubbles?	Cancelable?
blur	FocusEvent	Fires when an element loses focus either via the mouse or via tabbing	`Element` (except `<body>` and `<frameset>`), `Document`	No	No
focus	FocusEvent	Fires when an element receives focus	`Element` (except `<body>` and `<frameset>`), `Document`	No	No
focusin	FocusEvent	Fires when an event target is about to receive focus but before the focus is shifted; this event occurs right before the focus event	`Element`	Yes	No
focusout	FocusEvent	Fires when an event target is about to lose focus but before the focus is shifted; this event occurs right before the blur event	`Element`	Yes	No

Table 11-3. Form events

Event type	Event interface	Description	Event targets	Bubbles?	Cancelable?
change	Specific to HTML forms	Fires when a control loses the input focus and its value has been modified since gaining focus	Element	Yes	No
reset	Specific to HTML forms	Fires when a form is reset	Element	Yes	No
submit	Specific to HTML forms	Fires when a form is submitted	Element	Yes	Yes
select	Specific to HTML forms	Fires when a user selects some text in a text field, including input and textarea	Element	Yes	No

Table 11-4. Mouse events

Event type	Event interface	Description	Event targets	Bubbles?	Cancelable?
click	MouseEvent	Fires when a mouse pointer is clicked (or the user presses the Enter key) over an element. A click is defined as a mousedown and mouseup over the same screen location. The sequence of these events is mousedown>mouseup>click. Depending on the environment configuration, the click event may be dispatched if one or more of the event types mouseover, mouse move, and mouseout occur between the press and release of the pointing device button. The click event may also be followed by the dblclick event.	Element, Document, window	Yes	Yes
dblclick	MouseEvent	Fires when a mouse pointer is clicked twice over an element. The definition of a double-click depends on the environment configuration, except that the event target must be the same between mouse down, mouseup, and dblclick. This event type must be dispatched after the event type click if a click and double-click occur simultaneously, and after the event type mouseup otherwise.	Element, Document, window	Yes	Yes
mousedown	MouseEvent	Fires when a mouse pointer is pressed over an element.	Element, Document, window	Yes	Yes
mouseenter	MouseEvent	Fires when a mouse pointer is moved onto the boundaries of an element or one of its descendent elements. This event type is similar to mouse over, but differs in that it does not bubble and it must not be dispatched when the pointer device moves from an element onto the boundaries of one of its descendent elements.	Element, Document, window	No	No

Event type	Event interface	Description	Event targets	Bubbles?	Cancelable?
mouseleave	MouseEvent	Fires when a mouse pointer is moved off the boundaries of an element and all its descendent elements. This event type is similar to **mouse out**, but differs in that it does not bubble and it must not be dispatched until the pointing device has left the boundaries of the element and the boundaries of all its children.	Element, Document, window	No	No
mousemove	MouseEvent	Fires when a mouse pointer is moved while it is over an element. The frequency rate of events while the pointing device is moved is implementation-, device-, and platform-specific, but multiple consecutive **mousemove** events should be fired for sustained pointer-device movement, rather than a single event for each instance of mouse movement. Implementations are encouraged to determine the optimal frequency rate to balance responsiveness with performance.	Element, Document, window	Yes	No
mouseout	MouseEvent	Fires when a mouse pointer is moved off the boundaries of an element. This event type is similar to **mouseleave**, but differs in that it does bubble and it must be dispatched when the pointer device moves from an element onto the boundaries of one of its descendent elements.	Element, Document, window	Yes	Yes
mouseup	MouseEvent	Fires when a mouse pointer button is released over an element.	Element, Document, window	Yes	Yes
mouseover	MouseEvent	Fires when a mouse pointer is moved over an element.	Element, Document, window	Yes	Yes

Table 11-5. Wheel event

Event type	Event interface	Description	Event targets	Bubbles?	Cancelable?
wheel (browsers use mousewheel but the specification uses wheel)	WheelEvent	Fires when a mouse wheel has been rotated around any axis, or when an equivalent input device (such as a mouseball, certain tablets or touchpads, etc.) has emulated such an action. Depending on the platform and input device, diagonal wheel deltas may be delivered either as a single wheel event with multiple nonzero axes or as separate wheel events for each nonzero axis. Some helpful details about browser support can be found here (*http://bit.ly/YlZl84*).	Element, Document, window	Yes	Yes

Table 11-6. Keyboard events

Event type	Event interface	Description	Event targets	Bubbles?	Cancelable?
key down	KeyboardEvent	Fires when a key is initially pressed. This is sent after any key mapping is performed, but before any input method editors receive the keypress. This is sent for any key, even if it doesn't generate a character code.	Element, Document	Yes	Yes
key press	KeyboardEvent	Fires when a key is initially pressed, but only if that key normally produces a character value. This is sent after any key mapping is performed, but before any input method editors receive the keypress.	Element, Document	Yes	Yes
keyup	KeyboardEvent	Fires when a key is released. This is sent after any key mapping is performed, and always follows the corresponding **keydown** and **keypress** events.	Element, Document	Yes	Yes

Table 11-7. Touch events

Event type	Event interface	Description	Event targets	Bubbles?	Cancelable?
touchstart	TouchEvent	Fires an event to indicate when the user places a touch point on the touch surface	Element, Document, window	Yes	Yes
touchend	TouchEvent	Fires an event to indicate when the user removes a touch point (*http://www.w3.org/TR/2011/WD-touch-events-20110505/#dfn-touch-point*) from the touch surface, as well as cases where the touch point physically leaves the touch surface, such as being dragged off the screen	Element, Document, window	Yes	Yes
touchmove	TouchEvent	Fires an event to indicate when the user moves a touch point along the touch surface	Element, Document, window	Yes	Yes
touchenter	TouchEvent	Fires an event to indicate when a touch point moves onto the interactive area defined by a DOM element	Element, Document, window	No	N/A
touchleave	TouchEvent	Fires an event to indicate when a touch point moves off the interactive area defined by a DOM element	Element, Document, window	No	N/A
touchcancel	TouchEvent	Fires an event to indicate when a touch point has been disrupted in an implementation-specific manner, such as a synchronous event or action originating from the UA canceling the touch, or the touch point leaving the document window into a nondocument area that is capable of handling user interactions	Element, Document, window	Yes	No

Note
Touch events are typically only supported in iOS, Android, and Black-Berry browsers, or browsers that can switch on touch modes (e.g., Chrome).

Table 11-8. Window, <body>, and frame-specific events

Event type	Event interface	Description	Event targets	Bubbles?	Cancelable?
afterprint	N/A	Fires on the object immediately after its associated document prints or previews for printing	window, <body>, <frameset>	No	No
beforeprint	N/A	Fires on the object before its associated document prints or previews for printing	window, <body>, <frameset>	No	No
beforeunload	N/A	Fires prior to a document being unloaded	window, <body>, <frameset>	No	Yes
hashchange	HashChangeEvent	Fires when there are changes to the portion of a URL that follows the number sign (#)	window, <body>, <frameset>	No	No
message	N/A	Fires when the user sends a cross-document message or a message is sent from a Worker with postMessage	window, <body>, <frameset>	No	No
offline	NavigatorOffLine	Fires when the browser is working offline	window, <body>, <frameset>	No	No
online	NavigatorOnLine	Fires when the browser is working online	window, <body>, <frameset>	No	No
pagehide	PageTransitionEvent	Fires when a session history event is being traversed from	window, <body>, <frameset>	No	No
pageshow	PageTransitionEvent	Fires when a session history entry is being traversed to	window, <body>, <frameset>	No	No

Table 11-9. Document-specific events

Event type	Event interface	Description	Event targets	Bubbles?	Cancelable?
readystatechange	Event	Fires an event when `ready State` is changed	`Document`, `XMLHttpRe quest`	No	No
DOMContentLoaded	Event	Fires when a web page has been parsed, but before all resources have been fully downloaded	`Document`	Yes	No

Table 11-10. Drag events

Event type	Event interface	Description	Event targets	Bubbles?	Cancelable?
drag	DragEvent	Fires on the source object continuously during a drag operation.	`Element`, `Document`, `window`	Yes	Yes
dragstart	DragEvent	Fires on the source object when the user starts to drag a text selection or selected object. The `ondrag start` event is the first to fire when the user starts to drag the mouse.	`Element`, `Document`, `window`	Yes	Yes
dragend	DragEvent	Fires on the source object when the user releases the mouse at the close of a drag operation. The `ondragend` event is the final drag event to fire, following the `ondragleave` event, which fires on the target object.	`Element`, `Document`, `window`	Yes	No
dragenter	DragEvent	Fires on the target element when the user drags the object to a valid drop target.	`Element`, `Document`, `window`	Yes	Yes
dragleave	DragEvent	Fires on the target object when the user moves the mouse out of a valid drop target during a drag operation.	`Element`, `Document`, `window`	Yes	No
dragover	DragEvent	Fires on the target element continuously while the user drags the object over a valid drop target. The `on dragover` event fires on the target object after the `ondragenter` event has fired.	`Element`, `Document`, `window`	Yes	Yes
drop	DragEvent	Fires on the target object when the mouse button is released during a drag-and-drop operation. The `on drop` event fires before the `ondragleave` and `ondragend` events.	`Element`, `Document`, `window`	Yes	Yes

Notes

Tables 11-1 through 11-10 were crafted from the following resources: Document Object Model (DOM) Level 3 Events Specification 5 User Event Module (*http://bit.ly/WYNJZv*), DOM event reference (*http://mzl.la/12fpBaY*), HTML Living Standard 7.1.6 Event handlers on elements, Document objects, and Window objects (*http://bit.ly/Xt8lcj*), and Event compatibility tables (*http://bit.ly/TlScYl*).

In this section, I've only mentioned the most common event types. Keep in mind that there are numerous HTML5 APIs that I've excluded from this section, among them, media events (*http://bit.ly/U8J1fj*) for `<video>` and `<audio>` elements as well as all state change events for XMLHttpRequest Level 2 (*http://bit.ly/14DtF4h*).

The `copy`, `cut`, and `textinput` events are not defined by DOM3 events or HTML5.

Use `mouseenter` and `mouseleave` instead of `mouseover` and `mouseout`. Unfortunately, Chrome and Safari still haven't added these events!

11.3 The Event Flow

When an event is invoked, the event flows or propagates through the DOM (*http://bit.ly/XYlGbB*), firing the same event on other nodes and JavaScript objects. The event flow can be programmed to occur as a capture phase (i.e., DOM tree trunk to branches) or as a bubbling phase (i.e., DOM tree branches to trunk), or both.

In the following code, I set up 10 event listeners that can all be invoked, due to the event flow, by clicking once on the `<div>` element in the HTML document. When the `<div>` is clicked, the capture phase begins at the `window` object and propagates down the DOM tree firing the `click` event for each object (i.e., `window > document > <html> ><body> >` event target) until it hits the event target. Once the capture phase ends, the target phase starts, firing the `click` event on the target element itself. Next, the propagation phase propagates up from the event target firing the `click` event until it reaches the `window` object (i.e., event target > `<body>` > `<html>` > `document` > `window`). With this knowledge, it should be obvious why clicking the `<div>` in the code example logs to the console 1,2,3,4,5,6,7,8,9,10.

Live code (*http://jsfiddle.net/domenlightenment/CAdTv*)

```
<!DOCTYPE html>
<html lang="en">
<body>

<div>click me to start event flow</div>

<script>
```

```
/* notice that I am passing the addEventListener() a boolean parameter of true so
capture events fire, not just bubbling events */

//1 capture phase
window.addEventListener('click',function(){console.log(1);},true);

//2 capture phase
document.addEventListener('click',function(){console.log(2);},true);

//3 capture phase
document.documentElement.addEventListener
  ('click',function(){console.log(3);},true);

//4 capture phase
document.body.addEventListener('click',function(){console.log(4);},true);

//5 target phase occurs during capture phase
document.querySelector('div').addEventListener
  ('click',function(){console.log(5);},true);

//6 target phase occurs during bubbling phase
document.querySelector('div').addEventListener
  ('click',function(){console.log(6);},false);

//7 bubbling phase
document.body.addEventListener('click',function(){console.log(7);},false);

//8 bubbling phase
document.documentElement.addEventListener
  ('click',function(){console.log(8);},false);

//9 bubbling phase
document.addEventListener('click',function(){console.log(9);},false);

//10 bubbling phase
window.addEventListener('click',function(){console.log(10)},false);

</script>
</body>
</html>
```

After the <div> is clicked, the event flow proceeds in this order:

1. Capture phase invokes click events on window that are set to fire on capture

2. Capture phase invokes click events on document that are set to fire on capture

3. Capture phase invokes click events on <html> element that are set to fire on capture

4. Capture phase invokes click events on <body> element that are set to fire on capture

5. Target phase invokes click events on <div> element that are set to fire on capture

6. Target phase invokes click events on `<div>` element that are set to fire on bubble

7. Bubbling phase invokes click events on `<body>` element that are set to fire on bubble

8. Bubbling phase invokes click events on `<html>` element that are set to fire on bubble

9. Bubbling phase invokes click events on `document` that are set to fire on bubble

10. Bubbling phase invokes click events on `window` that are set to fire on bubble

The use of the capture phase is not all that common, due to a lack of browser support for this phase. Typically, events are assumed to be invoked during the bubbling phase. In the following code, I remove the capture phase from the previous code example and demonstrate what is usually occurring during an event invocation.

Live code (*http://jsfiddle.net/domenlightenment/C6qmZ*)

```
<!DOCTYPE html>
<html lang="en">
<body>

<div>click me to start event flow</div>

<script>

//1 target phase occurs during bubbling phase
document.querySelector('div').addEventListener('click',function()
    {console.log(1);},false);

//2 bubbling phase
document.body.addEventListener('click',function(){console.log(2);},false);

//3 bubbling phase
document.documentElement.addEventListener('click',function()
    {console.log(3);},false);

//4 bubbling phase
document.addEventListener('click',function(){console.log(4);},false);

//5 bubbling phase
window.addEventListener('click',function(){console.log(5)},false);

</script>
</body>
</html>
```

Notice in the last code example that if the click event is initiated on the `<body>` element (a click anywhere except on the `<div>`), the click event attached to the `<div>` is not invoked and bubbling invocation starts on the `<body>`. This is because the event target is no longer the `<div>` but rather is the `<body>` element.

Notes

Modern browsers do support the use of the capture phase, so what was once considered unreliable might just serve some value today. For example, one could intercept an event before it occurs on the event target.

Keep this knowledge of event capturing and bubbling at the forefront of your thoughts when you read the event delegation section of this chapter.

The event object passed to event listener functions has an eventPhase property containing a number that indicates in which phase an event is invoked. A value of 1 indicates the capture phase. A value of 2 indicates the target phase. And a value of 3 indicates the bubbling phase.

11.4 Adding Event Listeners to Element Nodes, the window Object, and the document Object

The addEventListener() method is available on all Element nodes, the window object, and the document object, providing the ability to add event listeners to parts of an HTML document as well as JavaScript objects relating to the DOM and the Browser Object Model [or BOM (*http://mzl.la/11dh48Y*)]. In the following code, I leverage this method to add a mousemove event to a <div> element, the document object, and the window object. Notice, due to the event flow, that mouse movement specifically over the <div> will invoke all three listeners each time a movement occurs.

Live code (*http://jsfiddle.net/domenlightenment/sSFK5*)

```
<!DOCTYPE html>
<html lang="en">

<body>

<div>mouse over me</div>

<script>

/* add a mousemove event to the window object, invoking the event during the
bubbling phase */
window.addEventListener('mousemove',function()
  {console.log('moving over window');},false);

/* add a mousemove event to the document object, invoking the event during the
bubbling phase */
document.addEventListener('mousemove',function()
  {console.log('moving over document');},false);

/* add a mousemove event to a <div> element object, invoking the event during the
bubbling phase */
```

```
document.querySelector('div').addEventListener('mousemove',function()
  {console.log('moving over div');},false);

</script>
</body>
</html>
```

The addEventListener() method used in the preceding code example takes three arguments. The first argument is the type of event to listen for. Notice that the event type string does not contain the "on" prefix (i.e., onmousemove) that event handlers require. The second argument is the function to be invoked when the event occurs. The third parameter is a Boolean indicating whether the event should be fired during the capture phase or the bubbling phase of the event flow.

Notes

I've purposely avoided discussing inline event handlers and property event handlers in favor of promoting the use of addEventListener().

Typically, a developer wants events to fire during the bubbling phase so that object eventing handles the event before bubbling the event up the DOM. Because of this, you almost always provide a false value as the last argument to the addEventListener(). In modern browsers, if the third parameter is not specified, it will default to false.

You should be aware that the addEventListener() method can be used on the XMLHttpRequest object.

11.5 Removing Event Listeners

The removeEventListener() method can be used to remove event listeners, if the original listener was not added using an anonymous function. In the following code, I add two event listeners to the HTML document and attempt to remove both of them. However, only the listener that was attached using a function reference is removed.

Live code (*http://jsfiddle.net/domenlightenment/XP2Ug*)

```
<!DOCTYPE html>
<html lang="en">
<body>

<div>click to say hi</div>

<script>

var sayHi = function(){console.log('hi')};

//adding event listener using anonymous function
document.body.addEventListener('click',function(){console.log('dude');},false);
```

```
//adding event listener using function reference
document.querySelector('div').addEventListener('click',sayHi,false);

/* attempt to remove both event listeners, but only the listener added with a
function reference is removed */
document.querySelector('div').removeEventListener('click',sayHi,false);

/* this of course does not work as the function passed to removeEventListener is a
new and different function */
document.body.removeEventListener('click',function(){console.log('dude');},false);

/* clicking the div will still invoke the click event attached to the body
element, this event was not removed */

</script>
</body>
</html>
```

Anonymous functions added using the `addEventListener()` method simply cannot be removed.

11.6 Getting Event Properties from the Event Object

By default, the handler or callback function invoked for events is sent a parameter that contains all relevant information about the event itself. In the following code, I demonstrate access to this event object and log all its properties and values for a load event as well as a click event. Make sure you click the <div> to see the properties associated with a click event.

Live code (*http://jsfiddle.net/domenlightenment/d4SnQ*)

```
<!DOCTYPE html>
<html lang="en">
<body>

<div>click me</div>

<script>

document.querySelector('div').addEventListener('click',function(event){
Object.keys(event).sort().forEach(function(item){
    console.log(item+' = '+event[item]); //logs event properties and values
});
},false);

//assumes 'this' is window
this.addEventListener('load',function(event){
Object.keys(event).sort().forEach(function(item){
    console.log(item+' = '+event[item]); //logs event properties and values
});
```

```
},false);

</script>
</body>
</html>
```

Keep in mind that each event will contain slightly different properties based on the event type—for example, `MouseEvent` (*http://mzl.la/14Dva2A*), `KeyboardEvent` (*http://mzl.la/14veold*), and `WheelEvent` (*http://mzl.la/VzJYxC*).

 Notes

The event object also provides the `stopPropagation()`, `stopImmedia tePropagation()`, and `preventDefault()` methods.

In this book, I use the argument name `event` to reference the event object. In truth, you can use any name you like, and it's not uncommon to see `e` or `evt`.

11.7 The Value of this When Using addEventListener()

The value of `this` inside the event listener function passed to the `addEventListen er()` method will be a reference to the node or object the event is attached to. In the following code, I attach an event to a `<div>` and then use `this` inside the event listener to gain access to the `<div>` element the event is attached to.

Live code (*http://jsfiddle.net/domenlightenment/HwKgH*)

```
<!DOCTYPE html>
<html lang="en">
<body>

<div>click me</div>

<script>

document.querySelector('div').addEventListener('click',function(){
// 'this' will be the element or node the event listener is attached to
console.log(this); //logs '<div>'
},false);

</script>
</body>
</html>
```

When events are invoked as part of the event flow, the `this` value will continue to be the value of the node or object that the event listener is attached to. In the following code, I add a `click` event listener to the `<body>`, and regardless of whether you click on the `<div>` or the `<body>`, the value of `this` always points to `<body>`.

```
<!DOCTYPE html>
<html lang="en">
<body>

<div>click me</div>

<script>

/* click on the <div> or the <body> the value of this remains the <body>
element node */
document.body.addEventListener('click',function(){
console.log(this); //log <body>...</body>
},false);

</script>
</body>
</html>
```

Additionally, it's possible using the event.currentTarget property to get the same reference, to the node or object invoking the event listener, that the this property provides. In the following code, I leverage the event.currentTarget event object property showcasing that it returns the same value as this.

```
<!DOCTYPE html>
<html lang="en">
<body>

<div>click me</div>

<script>

document.addEventListener('click',function(event){
console.log(event.currentTarget);  //logs '#document'
//same as...
console.log(this);
},false);

document.body.addEventListener('click',function(event){
console.log(event.currentTarget); //logs '<body>'
//same as...
console.log(this);
},false);

document.querySelector('div').addEventListener('click',function(event){
console.log(event.currentTarget); //logs '<div>'
//same as...
console.log(this);
},false);
```

```
</script>
</body>
</html>
```

11.8 Referencing the target of an Event and Not the Node or Object on Which the Event Is Invoked

Because of the event flow, it's possible to click a `<div>` contained inside a `<body>` element and have a `click` event listener attached to the `<body>` element get invoked. When this happens, the event object passed to the event listener function attached to the `<body>` provides a reference (i.e., `event.target`) to the node or object that the event originated on (i.e., the target). In the following code, when the `<div>` is clicked, the `<body>` element's `click` event listener is invoked, and the `event.target` property references the original `<div>` that was the target of the click event. The `event.target` can be extremely useful when an event fires, because the event flow needs knowledge about the origin of the event.

Live code (*http://jsfiddle.net/domenlightenment/dGkTQ*)

```
<!DOCTYPE html>
<html lang="en">
<body>

<div>click me</div>

<script>

document.body.addEventListener('click',function(event){
/* when the <div> is clicked logs '<div>' because the <div> was the target in
the event flow */
console.log(event.target);
},false);

</script>
</body>
</html>
```

Consider that, in our code example, if the `<body>` element is clicked instead of the `<div>`, the event `target` and the element node that the event listener is invoked on are the same. Therefore, `event.target`, `this`, and `event.currentTarget` will all contain a reference to the `<body>` element.

11.9 Using preventDefault() to Cancel Default Browser Events

Browsers provide several events already wired up when an HTML page is presented to a user. For example, clicking a link has a corresponding event (i.e., you navigate to a URL). So does clicking a checkbox (i.e., a box is checked) or typing text into a text field (i.e., text is input and appears on the screen). These browser events can be prevented by calling the preventDefault() method inside the event handler function associated with a node or object that invokes a browser default event. In the following code, I prevent the default event that occurs on <a>, <input>, and <textarea>.

Live code (*http://jsfiddle.net/domenlightenment/Ywcyh*)

```
<!DOCTYPE html>
<html lang="en">
<body>

<a href="google.com">no go</div>

<input type="checkbox" />

<textarea></textarea>

<script>

document.querySelector('a').addEventListener('click',function(event){
event.preventDefault(); /* stop the default event for <a>, which would be to load
                           a url */
},false);

document.querySelector('input').addEventListener('click',function(event){
event.preventDefault(); /* stop default event for checkbox, which would be to
                           toggle checkbox state */
},false);

document.querySelector('textarea').addEventListener('keypress',function(event){
event.preventDefault(); /* stop default event for textarea, which would be to add
                           characters typed */
},false);

/* keep in mind that events still propagate, clicking the link in this html
document will stop the default event but not event bubbling */
document.body.addEventListener('click',function(){
console.log('the event flow still flows!');
},false);

</script>
</body>
</html>
```

All attempts to click the link, check the box, or type in the text input area in the preceding code example will fail because I am preventing the default events for these elements from occurring.

Notes

The preventDefault() method does not stop events from propagating (i.e., bubbling or capture phases).

Providing a return false at the end of the body of the event listener has the same result as calling the preventDefault() method.

The event object passed to event listener functions contains a Boolean cancelable property that indicates whether the event will respond to the preventDefault() method and cancel the default behavior.

The event object passed to event listener functions contains a default Prevented property that indicates true if preventDefault() has been invoked for a bubbling event.

11.10 Using stopPropagation() to Stop the Event Flow

Calling stopPropagation() from within an event handler/listener will stop the capture and bubble event flow phases, but any events directly attached to the node or object will still be invoked. In the following code, the onclick event attached to the <body> never gets invoked, because we are stopping the event from bubbling up the DOM when clicking on the <div>.

Live code (*http://jsfiddle.net/domenlightenment/RFKmA*)

```
<!DOCTYPE html>
<html lang="en">
<body>

<div>click me</div>

<script>

document.querySelector
console.log('me too, b
},false);

document.querySelector
console.log('invoked al
  bubble event phases')
event.stopPropagation()
},false);

document.querySelector(
console.log('me too, bu
```

```
},false);

/* when the <div> is clicked, this event is not invoked because one of the events
attached to the <div> stops the capture and bubble flow. */
document.body.addEventListener('click',function(){
console.log('What, denied from being invoked!');
},false);

</script>
</body>
</html>
```

Notice that other click events attached to the <div> still get invoked! Additionally, using stopPropagation() does not prevent default events. Had the <div> in our code example been an <a> with an href value, calling stopPropagation would not have stopped the browser default events from getting invoked.

11.11 Using stopImmediatePropagation() to Stop the Event Flow As Well As Other Like Events on the Same Target

Calling stopImmediatePropagation() from within an event handler/listener will stop the event flow phases (i.e., stopPropagation()), as well as any other like events attached to the event target that are attached after the event listener that invokes the stopImmediatePropagation() method. In the following code example, if I call stopImmediatePropagation() from the second event listener attached to the <div>, the click event that follows will not get invoked.

Live code (*http://jsfiddle.net/domenlightenment/znSjM*)

```
<!DOCTYPE html>
<html lang="en">
<body>

<div>click me</div>

<script>

//first event attached
document.querySelector('div').addEventListener('click',function(){
console.log('I get invoked because I was attached first');
},false);

//second event attached
document.querySelector('div').addEventListener('click',function(event){
console.log('I get invoked, but stop any other click events on this target');
event.stopImmediatePropagation();
},false);
```

```
/* third event attached, but because stopImmediatePropagation() was called above
this event does not get invoked */
document.querySelector('div').addEventListener('click',function(){
console.log('I get stopped from the previous click event listener');
},false);

/* notice that the event flow is also cancelled as if stopPropagation was
called too */
document.body.addEventListener('click',function(){
console.log('What, denied from being invoked!');
},false);

</script>
</body>
</html>
```

Note

Using `stopImmediatePropagation()` does not prevent default events. Browser default events still get invoked, and only calling `preventDe fault()` will stop these events.

11.12 Custom Events

A developer is not limited to the predefined event types. It's possible to attach and invoke a custom event, using the `addEventListener()` method like normal in combination with `document.createEvent()`, `initCustomEvent()`, and `dispatchEvent()`. In the following code, I create a custom event called `goBigBlue` and invoke that event.

Live code (*http://jsfiddle.net/domenlightenment/fRndj*)

```
<!DOCTYPE html>
<html lang="en">
<body>

<div>click me</div>

<script>

var divElement = document.querySelector('div');

//create the custom event
var cheer = document.createEvent('CustomEvent'); /* the 'CustomEvent' parameter
                                                    is required */

//create an event listener for the custom event
divElement.addEventListener('goBigBlue',function(event){
    console.log(event.detail.goBigBlueIs)
},false);
```

```
/* Use the initCustomEvent method to set up the details of the custom event.
Parameters for initCustomEvent are: (event, bubble?, cancelable?, pass values
to event.detail) */
cheer.initCustomEvent('goBigBlue',true,false,{goBigBlueIs:'its gone!'});

//invoke the custom event using dispatchEvent
divElement.dispatchEvent(cheer);

</script>
</body>
</html>
```

Notes

IE 9 requires the fourth parameter on initCustomEvent(). It is not optional.

The DOM4 specification added a CustomEvent() constructor (*http://bit.ly/YoOXy9*) that has simplified the life cycle of a custom event, but it's not supported in IE 9, and as of this writing, it is still in flux.

11.13 Simulating/Triggering Mouse Events

Simulating an event is not unlike creating a custom event. In the case of simulating a mouse event, we create a MouseEvent by using document.createEvent(). Then, using initMouseEvent(), we set up the mouse event that is going to occur. Next, the mouse event is dispatched on the element on which we'd like to simulate an event (i.e., the <div> in the HTML document). In the following code, a click event is attached to the <div> in the page. Instead of clicking the <div> to invoke the click event, the event is triggered or simulated by programmatically setting up a mouse event and dispatching the event to the <div>.

Live code (*http://jsfiddle.net/domenlightenment/kx7zJ*)

```
<!DOCTYPE html>
<html lang="en">
<body>

<div>no need to click, we programmatically trigger it</div>

<script>

var divElement = document.querySelector('div');

//setup click event that will be simulated
divElement.addEventListener('click',function(event){
    console.log(Object.keys(event));
},false);
```

```
//create simulated mouse event 'click'
var simulateDivClick = document.createEvent('MouseEvents');

/* setup simulated mouse 'click'
initMouseEvent(type,bubbles,cancelable,view,detail,screenx,screeny,clientx,clienty,
ctrlKey,altKey,shiftKey,metaKey,button,relatedTarget) */
simulateDivClick.initMouseEvent(
  'click',true,true,document.defaultView,0,0,0,0,0,false,false,false,0,null,null);

//invoke simulated clicked event
divElement.dispatchEvent(simulateDivClick);

</script>
</body>
</html>
```

Note

As of this writing, simulating/triggering mouse events works in all modern browsers. Simulating other event types quickly becomes more complicated, and leveraging simulate.js (*http://bit.ly/11dhFI2*) or jQuery (e.g., the jQuery `trigger()` method) becomes necessary.

11.14 Event Delegation

Event delegation, stated simply, is the programmatic act of leveraging the event flow and a single event listener to deal with multiple event targets. A side effect of event delegation is that the event targets don't have to be in the DOM when the event is created in order for the targets to respond to the event. This is, of course, rather handy when dealing with XHR responses that update the DOM. By implementing event delegation, new content that is added to the DOM post JavaScript load parsing can immediately start responding to events. Imagine we have a table with an unlimited number of rows and columns. Using event delegation, we can add a single event listener to the `<table>` node that acts as a delegate for the node or object that is the initial target of the event. In the following code example, clicking any of the `<td>`s (i.e., the target of the event) will delegate its event to the `click` listener on the `<table>`. Don't forget, this is all made possible because of the event flow, and in this specific case, the bubbling phase.

Live code (*http://jsfiddle.net/domenlightenment/BRkVL*)

```
<!DOCTYPE html>
<html lang="en">
<body>

<p>Click a table cell</p>
```

```
<table border="1">
    <tbody>
        <tr><td>row 1 column 1</td><td>row 1 column 2</td></tr>
        <tr><td>row 2 column 1</td><td>row 2 column 2</td></tr>
        <tr><td>row 3 column 1</td><td>row 3 column 2</td></tr>
        <tr><td>row 4 column 1</td><td>row 4 column 2</td></tr>
        <tr><td>row 5 column 1</td><td>row 5 column 2</td></tr>
        <tr><td>row 6 column 1</td><td>row 6 column 2</td></tr>
    </tbody>
</table>

<script>

document.querySelector('table').addEventListener('click',function(event){
    if(event.target.tagName.toLowerCase() === 'td'){ /* make sure we only run code
                                                         if a td is the target */
        console.log(event.target.textContent); /* use event.target to gain access
                                                   to target of the event which is
                                                   the td */

    }
},false);

</script>
</body>
</html>
```

If we were to update the table in the code example with new rows, the new rows would respond to the click event as soon as they were rendered to the screen, because the click event is delegated to the <table> element node.

Note
Event delegation is ideally leveraged when you are dealing with a click, mousedown, mouseup, keydown, keyup, and keypress event type.

Creating dom.js: A Wishful jQuery-Inspired DOM Library for Modern Browsers

12.1 dom.js Overview

I want you to take the information and knowledge from this book and leverage it as I walk you through a foundation for a wishful, modern, jQuery-like DOM library called dom.js. Think of dom.js as the foundation to a modern library for selecting DOM nodes and doing something with them. Not unlike jQuery, the dom.js code will provide a function for selecting something from the DOM (or creating something) and then doing something with it. Here are some examples of the dom() function that shouldn't look all that foreign if you are familiar with jQuery or any DOM utility for selecting elements.

```
/* select in a document all li's in the first ul and get the innerHTML for the
first li */
dom('li','ul').html();

//create html structure using a document fragment and get the innerHTML of ul
dom('<ul><li>hi</li></ul>').html()
```

For most readers, this chapter is simply an exercise in taking the information in this book and applying it to a JavaScript DOM library. For others, this might just shed some light on jQuery itself and any DOM manipulation logic used in JavaScript frameworks today. Ideally, in the end, I hope this exercise inspires readers to craft their own micro-DOM abstractions on an as-needed basis when the situation is right. With that said, let's begin.

12.2 Creating a Unique Scope

To protect our dom.js code from the global scope, I will first create a unique scope within which it can live and operate without fear of collisions in the global scope. In the following code, I set up a pretty standard Immediately-Invoked Function Expression (*http://bit.ly/XcFZ4q*) to create this private scope. When the IIFE is invoked, the value of global will be set to the current global scope (i.e., window).

GitHub code (*https://github.com/codylindley/domjs/blob/master/builds/dom.js*)

```
(function(win){

var global = win;
var doc = this.document;

}}(window);
```

Inside the IIFE we set up a reference to the window and document objects (i.e., doc) to speed up access to these objects inside the IIFE.

12.3 Creating dom() and GetOrMakeDom(), Globally Exposing dom() and GetOrMakeDom.prototype

Just like we did with jQuery, we are going to create a function that will return a chainable, wrapped set (i.e., a custom array-like object) of DOM nodes (e.g., {0:ELEMENT_NODE, 1:ELEMENT_NODE,length:2}) based on the parameters sent into the function. In the following code, I set up the dom() function and parameters that get passed on to the GetOrMakeDOM constructor function that, when invoked, will return the object containing the DOM nodes that dom() then returns.

GitHub code (*https://github.com/codylindley/domjs/blob/master/builds/dom.js*)

```
(function(win){

var global = win;
var doc = global.document;

var dom = function(params,context){
    return new GetOrMakeDom(params,context);
};

var GetOrMakeDom = function(params,context){

};

})(window);
```

In order for the dom() function to be accessed/called from outside the private scope set up by the IIFE, we have to expose the function (i.e., create a reference) to the global scope. We do this by creating a property in the global scope, called dom, and pointing that property to the local dom() function. When dom is accessed from the global scope,

---

it will point to our locally scoped dom() function. In the following code, `global.dom = dom;` does the trick.

GitHub code (*https://github.com/codylindley/domjs/blob/master/builds/dom.js*)

```
(function(win){

var global = win;
var doc = global.document;
var dom = function(params,context){
    return new GetOrMakeDom(params,context);
};

var GetOrMakeDom = function(params,context){

};

//expose dom to global scope
global.dom = dom;

})(window);
```

The last thing we need to do is expose the `GetOrMakeDom.prototype` property to the global scope. As with jQuery (e.g., `jQuery.fn`), we are simply going to provide a shortcut reference from `dom.fn` to `GetOrMakeDOM.prototype`. This is shown in the following code.

```
(function(win){

var global = win;
var doc = global.document;
var dom = function(params,context){
    return new GetOrMakeDom(params,context);
};

var GetOrMakeDom = function(params,context){

};

//expose dom to global scope
global.dom = dom;

//short cut to prototype
dom.fn = GetOrMakeDom.prototype;

})(window);
```

Now anything attached to `dom.fn` is actually a property of the `GetOrMakeDOM.proto` type object and is inherited during property lookup for any object instance created from the `GetOrMakeDOM` constructor function.

Note

The getOrMakeDom function is invoked with the new operator. Make sure you understand what happens when a function is invoked using the new operator (*http://mzl.la/WYOJNp*).

12.4 Creating an Optional Context Parameter Passed to dom()

When dom() is invoked, it also invokes the GetOrMakeDom function, passing it the parameters that are sent to dom(). When the GetOrMakeDOM constructor is invoked the first thing we need to do is determine the context. The context for working with the DOM can be set by passing a selector string used to select a node or a node reference itself. Passing a context to the dom() function provides the ability to limit the search for element nodes to a specific branch of the DOM tree. This is almost identical to the second parameter passed to the jQuery or $ function. In the following code, I default the context to the current document found in the global scope. If a context parameter is available, I determine what it is (i.e., a string or node) and either make the node pass in the context or select a node via querySelectorAll().

GitHub code (*https://github.com/codylindley/domjs/blob/master/builds/dom.js*)

```
(function(win){

var global = win;
var doc = global.document;
var dom = function(params,context){
    return new GetOrMakeDom(params,context);
};

var GetOrMakeDom = function(params,context){

    var currentContext = doc;
        if(context){
            if(context.nodeType){//it's either a document node or element node
                currentContext = context;
            }else{ //else it's a string selector, use it to select a node
                currentContext = doc.querySelector(context);
        }
    }

};

//expose dom to global scope
global.dom = dom;
```

```
//shortcut to prototype
dom.fn = GetOrMakeDom.prototype;

})(window);
```

With the `context` parameter logic set up, we can next add the logic required to deal with the `params` parameter used to actually select or create nodes.

12.5 Populating an Object with DOM Node References Based on params and a Return Object

The type of `params` parameter passed to `dom()`, and then on to `getOrMakeDom()`, varies. Similar to jQuery, the types of values passed can be any one of the following:

- CSS selector string (e.g., dom('body'))
- HTML string (e.g., dom('<p>Hello</p><p> World!</p>'))
- Element node (e.g., dom(document.body))
- Array of element nodes (e.g., dom([document.body]))
- A NodeList (e.g., dom(document.body.children))
- An HTMLcollection (e.g., dom(document.all))
- A dom() object itself (e.g., dom(dom()))

The result of passing `params` is the construction of a chainable object containing references to nodes (e.g., `{0:ELEMENT_NODE,1:ELEMENT_NODE,length:2}`) either in the DOM or in a document fragment. Let's examine how each of the aforementioned parameters can be used to produce an object containing node references.

The logic to permit such a wide variety of parameter types is shown in the following code and starts with a simple check to verify that `params` is not `undefined`, an empty string, or a string with empty spaces. If this is the case, we add a `length` property with a value of 0 to the object constructed from calling `GetOrMakeDOM` and return the object so that the execution of the function ends. If `params` is not a false or false-like value (*http://bit.ly/UJTHyO*), the execution of the function continues.

Next, the `params` value, if it is a string, is checked to see if it contains HTML. If the string contains HTML, a document fragment (*http://mzl.la/W7Wcds*) is created and the string is used as the `innerHTML` value for a `<div>` contained in the document fragment so that the string is converted to a DOM structure. With the HTML string converted to a node tree, the structure is looped over accessing top-level nodes, and references to these nodes are passed to the object being created by `GetOrMakeDom`. If the string does not contain HTML, execution of the function continues.

The next check simply verifies whether params is a reference to a single node, and if it is, we wrap a reference to it in an object and return it; otherwise, we are pretty sure the params value is an HTML collection (*http://mzl.la/11degsA*), node list (*http://mzl.la/YJ06hh*), array, string selector (*http://bit.ly/W7WpNN*), or object created from dom(). If it's a string selector, a node list is created by calling the querySelectorAll() method on the currentContext. If it's not a string selector, we loop over the HTML collection, node list, array, or object, extracting the node references and using the references as values contained in the object sent back from calling GetOrMakeDom.

All this logic inside the GetOrMakeDom() function can be a bit overwhelming; just realize that the point of the constructor function is to construct an object containing references to nodes (e.g., {0:ELEMENT_NODE,1:ELEMENT_NODE,length:2}) and return this object to dom().

GitHub code (*https://github.com/codylindley/domjs/blob/master/builds/dom.js*)

```
(function(win){

var global = win;
var doc = global.document;
var dom = function(params,context){
    return new GetOrMakeDom(params,context);
};

var regXContainsTag = /^\s*<(\w+|!)[^>]*>/;

var GetOrMakeDom = function(params,context){

    var currentContext = doc;
    if(context){
        if(context.nodeType){
            currentContext = context;
        }else{
            currentContext = doc.querySelector(context);
        }
    }

    //if no params, return empty dom() object
    if(!params || params === '' ||
      typeof params === 'string' && params.trim() === ''){
        this.length = 0;
        return this;
    }

    //if HTML string, construct domfragment, fill object, then return object
    if(typeof params === 'string' && regXContainsTag.test(params)){
        //yup it's for sure html string
        /* create div and docfrag, append div to docfrag, then set its div's inner
        HTML to the string, then get first child */
        var divElm = currentContext.createElement('div');
```

```
            divElm.className = 'hippo-doc-frag-wrapper';
            var docFrag = currentContext.createDocumentFragment();
            docFrag.appendChild(divElm);
            var queryDiv = docFrag.querySelector('div');
            queryDiv.innerHTML = params;
            var numberOfChildren = queryDiv.children.length;
            /* loop over nodelist and fill object, needs to be done because a string
            of html can be passed with siblings */
            for (var z = 0; z < numberOfChildren; z++) {
                this[z] = queryDiv.children[z];
            }
            //give the object a length value
            this.length = numberOfChildren;
            //return object
            return this; //return e.g. {0:ELEMENT_NODE,1:ELEMENT_NODE,length:2}
        }

        //if a single node reference is passed, fill object, return object
        if(typeof params === 'object' && params.nodeName){
            this.length = 1;
            this[0] = params;
            return this;
        }

        /* if it's an object but not a node assume nodelist or array, else it's a
        string selector, so create nodelist */
        var nodes;
        if(typeof params !== 'string'){//nodelist or array
            nodes = params;
        }else{//ok string
            nodes = currentContext.querySelectorAll(params.trim());
        }
        //loop over array or nodelist created above and fill object
        var nodeLength = nodes.length;
        for (var i = 0; i < nodeLength; i++) {
            this[i] = nodes[i];
        }
        //give the object a length value
        this.length = nodeLength;
        //return   object
        return this; //return e.g., {0:ELEMENT_NODE,1:ELEMENT_NODE,length:2}

    };

    //expose dom to global scope
    global.dom = dom;

    //shortcut to prototype
    dom.fn = GetOrMakeDom.prototype;

})(window);
```

12.6 Creating an each() Method and Making It a Chainable Method

When we invoke dom(), we can access anything attached to dom.fn by way of prototypical inheritance (e.g., dom().each()). Not unlike jQuery, methods attached to dom.fn operate on the object created from the GetOrMakeDom constructor function. The following code sets up the each() method.

GitHub code (*https://github.com/codylindley/domjs/blob/master/builds/dom.js*)

```
dom.fn.each = function (callback) {
    var len = this.length; /* the specific instance created from getOrMakeDom()
                              and returned by calling dom() */
    for(var i = 0; i < len; i++){
        /* invoke the callback function setting the value of this to element node
        and passing it parameters */
        callback.call(this[i], i, this[i]);
    }
}
```

As you might expect, the each() method takes a callback function as a parameter and invokes the function (setting the this value to the element node object with call()) for each node element in the getOrMakeDom object instance. The this value inside the each() function is a reference to the getOrMakeDom object instance (e.g., {0:ELEMENT_NODE,1:ELEMENT_NODE,length:2}).

When a method does not return a value (e.g., dom().length returns a length), it's possible to allow method chaining by simply returning the object the method belongs to instead of a specific value. Basically, we are returning the GetOrMakeDom object so that another method can be called on this instance of the object. In the following code, I would like the each() method to be chainable, meaning more methods can be called after calling each(), so I simply return this. The this in the code is the object instance created from calling the getOrMakeDom function.

GitHub code (*https://github.com/codylindley/domjs/blob/master/builds/dom.js*)

```
dom.fn.each = function (callback) {
    var len = this.length;
    for(var i = 0; i < len; i++){
        callback.call(this[i], i, this[i]);
    }
    return this; /* make it chainable by returning e.g.,
                   {0:ELEMENT_NODE,1:ELEMENT_NODE,length:2} */
};
```

12.7 Creating html(), append(), and text() Methods

With the core each() method created and implicit iteration available, we can now build out a few dom() methods that act on the nodes we select from an HTML document or that we create using document fragments. The three methods we are going to create are:

- html() / html('html string')
- text() / text('text string')
- append('html | text | dom() | nodelist/HTML collection | node | array')

The html() and text() methods follow a very similar pattern. If the method is called with a parameter value, we loop (using dom.fn.each() for implicit iteration) over each element node in the getOrMakeDom object instance, setting either the innerHTML value or the textContent value. If no parameter is sent, we simply return the innerHTML or textContent value for the first element node in the getOrMakeDom object instance. In the following example, you will see this logic coded.

GitHub code (*https://github.com/codylindley/domjs/blob/master/builds/dom.js*)

```
dom.fn.html = function(htmlString){
    if(htmlString){
        return this.each(function(){ /* notice I return this so it's chainable if
                                    called with param */
            this.innerHTML = htmlString;
        });
    }else{
        return this[0].innerHTML;
    }
};

dom.fn.text = function(textString){
    if(textString){
        return this.each(function(){ /* notice I return this so it's chainable if
                                    called with param */
            this.textContent = textString;
        });
    }else{
        return this[0].textContent.trim();
    }
};
```

The append() method leveraging insertAdjacentHTML will take an HTML string, text string, dom() object, node list/HTML collection, single node, or array of nodes and append it to the nodes that have been selected.

```
dom.fn.append = function(stringOrObject){
    return this.each(function(){
        if(typeof stringOrObject === 'string'){
            this.insertAdjacentHTML('beforeend',stringOrObject);
        }else{
            var that = this;
            dom(stringOrObject).each(function(name,value){
                that.insertAdjacentHTML('beforeend',value.outerHTML);
            });
        }
    });
};
```

12.8 Taking dom.js for a Spin

During the development of dom.js, I created some very simple QUnit tests (*https://github.com/codylindley/domjs/tree/master/test*) that we are now going to run outside the testing framework. However, you can also run the testing framework to see dom.js in action (*https://github.com/codylindley/domjs/blob/master/test/index.html*). The follow code demonstrates the code created in this chapter.

Live code (*http://jsfiddle.net/domenlightenment/7aqKm*)

```
<!DOCTYPE html>
<html lang="en">
<body>

<ul>
<li>1</li>
<li>2</li>
<li>3</li>
</ul>

<script src=
  "https://raw.github.com/codylindley/domjs/master/builds/dom.js">
</script>
<script>

//dom()
console.log(dom());
console.log(dom(''));
console.log(dom('body'));
console.log(dom('<p>Hello</p><p> World!</p>'));
console.log(dom(document.body));
console.log(dom([document.body, document.body]));
console.log(dom(document.body.children));
console.log(dom(dom('body')));
```

```
//dom().html()
console.log(dom('ul li:first-child').html('one'));
console.log(dom('ul li:first-child').html() === 'one');

//dom().text()
console.log(dom('ul li:last-child').text('three'));
console.log(dom('ul li:last-child').text() === 'three');

//dom().append()
dom('ul').append('<li>4</li>');
dom('ul').append(document.createElement('li'));
dom('ul').append(dom('li:first-child'));

</script>
</body>
</html>
```

12.9 Summary and Continuing with dom.js

This chapter was about creating a foundation to a jQuery-like DOM library. If you'd like to continue studying the building blocks to a jQuery-like DOM library, I suggest checking out hippo.js (*https://github.com/codylindley/hippojs*), which is an exercise in recreating the jQuery DOM methods for modern browsers. Both dom.js (*https://github.com/codylindley/domjs*) and hippo.js (*https://github.com/codylindley/hippojs*) make use of grunt (*http://gruntjs.com/*), QUnit (*http://qunitjs.com/*), and JS Hint (*http://jshint.com/*) which I highly recommend looking into if building your own JavaScript libraries is of interest. In addition to the aforementioned developer tools, I highly recommend reading "Designing Better JavaScript APIs" (*http://coding.smashingmaga zine.com/2012/10/09/designing-javascript-apis-usability/*). Now go build something for the DOM.

About the Author

Cody Lindley (*http://www.codylindley.com*) is a client-side engineer (a.k.a. frontend developer) and recovering Flash developer. He has an extensive background working professionally (11+ years) with HTML, CSS, JavaScript, Flash, and client-side performance techniques as they pertain to web development. If he is not wielding client-side code, he is likely toying with interface/interaction design or authoring material and speaking at various conferences. When not sitting in front of a computer, it is a sure bet he is hanging out with his wife and kids in Boise, Idaho—training for triathlons, skiing, mountain biking, road biking, alpine climbing, reading, watching movies, or debating the rational evidence for a Christian worldview.

Colophon

The animal on the cover of *DOM Enlightenment* is the Pemba Scops Owl (*Otus pembaensis*).

The cover image is from Bernard's *Histoire Naturelle*. The cover font is Adobe ITC Garamond. The text font is Adobe Minion Pro; the heading font is Adobe Myriad Condensed; and the code font is Dalton Maag's Ubuntu Mono.

Get even more for your money.

Join the O'Reilly Community, and register the O'Reilly books you own. It's free, and you'll get:

- $4.99 ebook upgrade offer
- 40% upgrade offer on O'Reilly print books
- Membership discounts on books and events
- Free lifetime updates to ebooks and videos
- Multiple ebook formats, DRM FREE
- Participation in the O'Reilly community
- Newsletters
- Account management
- 100% Satisfaction Guarantee

Signing up is easy:

1. **Go to: oreilly.com/go/register**
2. **Create an O'Reilly login.**
3. **Provide your address.**
4. **Register your books.**

Note: English-language books only

To order books online:

oreilly.com/store

For questions about products or an order:

orders@oreilly.com

To sign up to get topic-specific email announcements and/or news about upcoming books, conferences, special offers, and new technologies:

elists@oreilly.com

For technical questions about book content:

booktech@oreilly.com

To submit new book proposals to our editors:

proposals@oreilly.com

O'Reilly books are available in multiple DRM-free ebook formats. For more information:

oreilly.com/ebooks

Spreading the knowledge of innovators   oreilly.com

CPSIA information can be obtained at www.ICGtesting.com
Printed in the USA
LVOW012331150313

324588LV00007B/235/P